Oriental Living

GUILLAUME DE LAUBIER

DÉSIRÉE SADEK

Preface

In the heart of our world, where the threads of history are woven with the vibrancy of the present, lies a realm where the art of living finds its most profound expressions. *Oriental Living* is a homage to that realm—a celebration of the rich, intricate tapestry of Eastern aesthetics and the way they harmoniously blend with contemporary sensibilities.

The journey of creating this book has been one of enchantment and revelation, a pilgrimage through spaces where time stands still and yet whispers the secrets of ages past. Rooted in a deep reverence for cultural heritage, this collection pays tribute to the craftsmanship that defines Oriental art and design. From the storied palaces to the serene, sun-dappled gardens of Morocco, each page is a testament to the timeless beauty and enduring allure of these ancient traditions.

Lebanon, with its soul steeped in history and its spirit soaring towards the future, is a central muse in this journey. Here, amidst the bustling streets of Beirut and the tranquil valleys of the Bekaa, the old and the new dance in a delicate, perpetual embrace. This land, rich with stories carved in stone and whispered through cedar trees, serves as a vivid backdrop for many of the homes and spaces we explore. It is a place where the echoes of Phoenician traders mingle with the calls of contemporary artists, creating a symphony of sights and sounds that is uniquely Lebanese.

Oriental Living is not merely a collection of beautiful images; it is a narrative—a story brought to life through the lens of the talented photographer Guillaume de Laubier and the voices of the architects, designers, and homeowners who have poured their hearts into these spaces. Each home featured within these pages is more than a dwelling; it is a sanctuary where history and modernity meet, where antique treasures and contemporary design elements coexist in perfect harmony.

We invite you to wander through these inspired and inspiring places. Marvel at the seamless integration of antique artifacts with cutting-edge design, creating environments that are both nostalgic and innovative. Each visit is a portal to a different world, offering glimpses into the materials, techniques, and philosophies that have shaped these extraordinary interiors.

May *Oriental Living* inspire you to see the beauty in both the old and the new, to cherish the craftsmanship of the past, and to explore the endless possibilities of blending these influences in your own spaces. As you turn these pages, may you find not just ideas for decoration, but a deeper connection to the rich cultural legacies that have shaped our world.

Welcome to a journey through time and space, where every room tells a story, and every story adds a vibrant thread to the living tapestry of Oriental art and design.

Désirée Sadek

Table of Contents

08	**Art Living**
28	**Indira's Realm**
48	**Ochre Oasis**
66	**Blending Tradition and Modernity**
86	**The Happy Farm in the Valley**
106	**A Thousand and One Nights**
128	**The Governor's Palace**
146	**Pink Palm Grove**
166	**Bohemian Chic**
182	**The Gem of Marrakech**
204	**Spirit of the Past**
222	**Urban Loft**
236	**The Art and the Way**

Art Living

—⋅❯❯ ❮❮⋅—

Zoé and Nabil Debs are globetrotters on a unique mission: to discover and revitalise homes brimming with character, transforming them into exclusive guesthouses that serve as sanctuaries for contemporary art and offer a haven for travelers seeking the allure of beauty. These rejuvenated spaces are collectively known as Arthaus.

The Debs' family abode is a traditional Lebanese house, identifiable by its three arches and dating back to the latter half of the 19th century. Nestled in Beirut's vibrant Achrafieh district, this residence showcases a layout centered around a grand hall leading to adjoining rooms, graced by impressively tall ceilings. The original construction, attributed to Italian master masons, represents a blend of diverse influences, making it a quintessential Beirut home.

In a harmonious lounge setting, the enigmatic works of artist Sabhan Adam preside over the space, surrounded by iconic 1950s Italian armchairs adorned with plush yellow velvet. This exquisite blend of art and design encapsulates the vibrant spirit of the era, beckoning guests to contemplate and find comfort in their surroundings.

(previous page) The living room transports visitors through layers of history, with the 'Battle of Kulikovo' painting evoking the historic depth of Russia, complemented by the ancient allure of a circa 350 AD Roman mosaic. Beyond the walls, Nadim Karam's evocative 'Body and Soul' artwork animates the outdoor space, weaving together a narrative of art through the ages.

(right) In the bar area, a vintage early 1970s 'Flying Saucer' ceiling light casts a warm glow over an eclectic mix of art: a vivid painting by Cuban artist Alejandro Gómez Cangas, a captivating photo of Miami by Jorge Otero, and an ancient Roman bas-relief dating back to circa 250 AD. This unique blend of elements creates a timeless space where history and modernity converge effortlessly.

Oriental Living

During renovation, Zoé and Nabil opted for a bold structural modification: they created an opening that extends from the main living area to the first-floor galleries. This alteration not only enhanced the spatial volume but also introduced a modern flair, sacrificing some living space for the benefit of increased light and ventilation, thus revitalising the traditional Lebanese architecture.

The interior design philosophy was one of minimalism, where each room was stripped of unnecessary elements to foster a tranquil, Zen-like atmosphere. This approach created space to display art installations and pieces from the Debs' expansive collection, which grows daily with contributions from artists worldwide, notably from South America. Their collection also celebrates Lebanese artistry, featuring works by Habib Srour, Saliba Douaihy and Nadim Karam, among others, offering guests a unique lens through which to experience Beirut's cultural tapestry.

Expanding their vision further, the Debs added three new buildings across from their home, ingeniously blending traditional architecture with modernist designs. These additions boast an array of amenities including a panoramic bar, exhibition spaces, a swimming pool, and a lush garden with fruit trees, all encapsulating the essence of Achrafieh's vibrant heart.

The *original construction*, attributed to Italian master masons, represents a blend of *diverse influences*, making it a quintessential Beirut home

A stunning hallway in Arthaus highlights the seamless blend of historical and contemporary design. Traditional wooden double doors open to reveal an elegant corridor adorned with arched openings and intricate chandeliers. A rich, patterned rug leads the eye towards a sunlit dining area, while a mix of antique and modern decor, including a striking painting and sculptural pieces, creates a sophisticated ambiance.

The Debs' project stands as a testament to a harmonious blend where silence meets the city buzz, historic stones coalesce with sleek lines, vast openings juxtapose with hidden recesses, and contemporary art coexists with timeless antiques. This fusion mirrors the enchanting duality of Beirut itself, a city that perpetually captivates its visitors, residents, and those hopelessly in love with its charm.

Arthaus embodies the Debs' innovative approach to merging historical charm with contemporary elegance. Their work transcends mere renovation, transforming each property into a cultural nexus that showcases the dynamic interplay of art and architecture. Through their discerning eye, these spaces evolve into immersive experiences that reflect the multifaceted essence of Beirut. The Debs' projects feature unique homes across the globe, from the picturesque Thames riverside to the secret passageways of Havana, the mountainous terrains of Megève, and the quaint allure of Saint-Tropez. Renowned for revitalising spaces with meticulous design and a deep reverence for the arts, the Debs provide a unique window into the city's rich heritage and its vibrant present, creating a dialogue between the past and the future in every meticulously curated corner. —

(right) The staircase showcases their deep respect for heritage. Framed ancestral portraits by Lebanese artists line the walls, providing a connection to the past. The wrought-iron railing, paired with the warmth of wooden accents and a cozy yellow settee, invites a harmonious blend of tradition and modern comfort. This space elegantly bridges the home's historical elements with contemporary touches, creating a welcoming and culturally rich environment.

Oriental Living

(previous page) The St. Joseph le Damascene Suite pays tribute to the revered 19th-century archbishop and 1993 canonised martyr, St. Joseph of Damascus. Renowned for his translation of religious texts into Arabic and his advocacy for interfaith dialogue, his enduring legacy of scholarship and unity resonates through the ages. His tragic martyrdom at the hands of fanatic factions in 1860 serves as a poignant reminder of his profound influence. Adorned with vibrant frescoes by Cuban artist Renelio Marin, this suite immortalises his memory.

(right) Suite Basilios, named in honor of the esteemed Metropolitan Basilios (Al-Debs), bears homage to his illustrious leadership. From his tenure in New York and Montreal to his appointment as the Archbishop of Tripoli and Akkar in 1903, Metropolitan Basilios' legacy is one of cultural enrichment and spiritual guidance. Reflecting a blend of cultural heritage and contemporary artistry, the suite showcases paintings by Mohamed El Masri, Marwan Chamaa and Jorge Otero, including a striking portrayal of Beirut's iconic 'Egg' building. A sculpture by Lina Husseini infuses a modern aesthetic, enhancing the suite's ambiance with a touch of sophistication.

Oriental Living

(left) Suite Habib presents a heartfelt double tribute to Habib Debs, honoring both the grandfather and the elder brother (1958-2023), a visionary architect and urban planner renowned for his pivotal role in designing the contemporary Arthaus Beirut building.

(below) Suite Loulou is a tender homage to Elie Debs, the brother of Nabil Debs and an esteemed interior architect (1960-1996). The suite's decor features a captivating painting by Marwan Chamaa, featuring the iconic Casino du Liban.

Art Living

(right) On the western side, a serene pool area offers a tranquil escape, embodying the essence of relaxation and leisure. This oasis is a perfect blend of luxury and tranquility, inviting guests to unwind in its soothing waters beneath the open sky.

(below) The north Facade garden, deeply scarred by the Beirut port explosion, now stands resiliently adorned with Nadim Karam's sculpture 'Body and Soul'.

Indira's Realm

Located in Kfour, a scenic village 24 km northeast of Beirut in the Keserwan District, stands a delightful home steeped in two centuries of history. Recently renamed Indira, this residence has been transformed into a guest house that captures the spirit of the Orient.

Acquired in 1986, this Lebanese home, with a history spanning over 200 years, has undergone numerous renovations over the past four decades, breathing life into its walls, hosting countless gatherings, and accumulating many cherished memories. Today, it serves as a sanctuary for an eclectic art collection spanning cultures and regions, from the Middle East to East and Southeast Asia. Among its treasures are Damascene woodwork, vibrant Chinese portraits, collectibles, sculptures, carpets, manuscripts and original artworks, each contributing to its unique ambiance and purpose as a crossroads of civilisations and faiths.

Embracing its new identity as Indira, the residence reflects the owners' innovative response to periods of absence due to extensive travel. Recognising that a shuttered home swiftly loses its essence, they were inspired to repurpose it as a guest house, bestowing upon it the name Indira. The choice was deliberate, aimed at capturing the fusion of Eastern cultures in a name that is both pronounceable and imbued with a warm, feminine allure. Indira, derived from Sanskrit, signifies "splendid".

Explore the enchanting Indira guesthouse, a 200-year-old Lebanese marvel nestled in Kfour, where Oriental charm and modern luxury blend seamlessly within its historic walls.

Step into Indira and embark on a visual journey through diverse cultures, with its collection of Damascene woodwork, Chinese portraits, and unique art pieces from the Middle East to Southeast Asia.

Oriental Living

Oriental Living

This elegant space showcases the intricate beauty of Damascene woodwork, paired with plush velvet seating and vibrant cushions, epitomizing the fusion of traditional craftsmanship and modern comfort at Indira guest house.

(next page) In the dining room a crystal chandelier takes center stage, while at the distant end, a Damascene cabinet houses valuable silverware, creating an ambience of refined elegance.

Oriental Living

> Indira offers more than a place to stay; it provides a journey through *time* and *culture*, inviting visitors to *explore* the depths of *history* and human *creativity*

The vision for Indira was to create a confluence of historical and contemporary elements. This ambition was realised through a collaborative restoration effort, spearheaded by the renowned Maison Tarazi, specialists in oriental craftsmanship since 1862, and Carole Tarazi Nasnas, a dynamic fashion consultant turned interior designer. Isabelle Eddé, with her expertise in art and diplomacy, was appointed to oversee the guesthouse, ensuring Indira's hospitality remained both elegant and welcoming. The décor strategy aimed to blend antique items with modern designs, utilising a medley of velvet sofas, silk pillows, and vibrant linens to adorn the communal spaces and suites. The color palette ranged from indoor blues and greens to outdoor pastels and vibrant hues, complemented by wooden and stonework textures, and accented with reds, oranges, Ottoman tulip chandeliers, and mother-of-pearl inlay.

The crown jewel of Indira is its iconic stone-vaulted gallery, once a stable, now reimagined as a piano bar. Its remarkable size and distinctive architecture, featuring a series of unique windows and intersecting vaults, captivate all who enter. The meticulous blend of historical charm and modern luxury, alongside a commitment to comfort, pleasure, and fine dining, sets Indira apart as a testament to exceptional hospitality.

Indira stands not only as a testament to architectural beauty and cultural fusion, but also as an oasis of tranquility and inspiration. Every corner tells a story, and every artifact echoes the travels and tales of distant lands. —

(right) Enter a royal bedroom adorned with an antique Otoman chandelier on the ceiling, magnificent engravings on the walls and a bed designed by Carole Tarazi Nasnas.

(next page) Marvel at the transformation of Indira's stone-vaulted gallery, once a stable, now an exquisite piano bar, showcasing architectural brilliance and inviting moments of musical bliss.

Ochre Oasis

Nestled within the tranquil landscapes of Morocco, this home unveils a story in every nook and cranny, beckoning exploration amidst the enduring allure of local design. The decision to dress the home in a singular shade of ochre was a thoughtful decision by the owners, symbolising simplicity, authenticity, and an impeccable aesthetic deeply rooted in its Moroccan context.

The story begins with a 4-hectare plot of land, where a small farm sits at the crossroads of the Ourika and Ouarzazate roads, a territory rarely explored by foreigners. This land, inhabited by cows, sheep, a smattering of olive and fig trees, and a solitary palm tree, did not deter Héléna Paraboschi and Pierre Pirajean. Despite its lack of appeal to the typical Morocco enthusiasts, the couple was captivated by its wild yet serene nature. With a proven track record for identifying emerging hotspots from Ibiza to Paris, and from Dubai to Marrakech, the couple embarked on transforming the area into a sought-after destination.

An intimate alcove within the ochre abode showcases the beauty of traditional Moroccan design. The earthy tones of the walls, accented by subtle lighting, create a warm and inviting atmosphere. The handcrafted mirror and vintage chairs add a touch of rustic elegance, reflecting the owners' commitment to authenticity and craftsmanship.

The expansive designer sofas merge seamlessly with the setting, accompanied by Studio Hopscotch London coffee tables and bespoke resin lamps adorned with gold and copper leaf patina.

An elegant sculpture by the owner stands poised, perfectly capturing the blend of modern art and rustic charm. The backdrop of natural wood and soft drapery enhances the room's serene ambiance, while the mirror cleverly reflects the statue, creating a sense of depth and continuity throughout the space.

Decorating this house in *shades* that match the *dominant ochre* color scheme was a deliberate choice by the owners, embodying *simplicity*, *authenticity*, and *impeccable presentation*

The kitchen welcomes visitors with a stately wooden door and an elegant alabaster lighting fixture.

> For the *interior design*, the couple turned to Studio Pirajean Lees, founded by their eldest daughter and son-in-law, based in London, adding a *personal touch* and blending *contemporary* and *traditional aesthetics*

A year of collaboration with architect Hakim Benjelloun, followed by another year sourcing deals with Tajdid Assala, a firm that specialises in riad restoration, brought the couple's vision to life. Their instructions were clear: prioritize the outdoors and natural surroundings. This led to the selection of subdued earthy tones, natural materials like wood, tadelakt, and stone, and a commitment to traditional craftsmanship. Additionally, they insisted that the structure should not overshadow the mature trees on the property. For the interior design, the couple turned to Studio Pirajean Lees, founded by their eldest daughter and son-in-law, based in London, adding a personal touch and blending contemporary and traditional aesthetics.

By the end of 2005, their dream residence had become a reality, spanning 800 square meters on a single floor. Featuring seven bedrooms—two of which are in a detached guest house with a private terrace—a spacious living room with oversized sofas, a dining area, a studio, and a 30-metre swimming pool, it perfectly balances modesty with abundance. "The custom doors and shutters were crafted by a carpenter, using the finest woods from the local palm groves. While our initial decor choice remains unchanged, we're committed to preserving the house's natural allure and craftsmanship."

This haven of tranquility not only stands as a testament to the couple's vision but also serves as a beacon of inspiration for those who seek to blend traditional aesthetics with contemporary comfort. The meticulous attention to detail and dedication to preserving the essence of Moroccan craftsmanship have created a space that is more than just a house, but a home that tells a story of adventure, discovery, and a profound connection to the land. As the seasons change, the ochre abode evolves, a timeless reminder of the symbiosis between nature and human creativity. —

A beautifully carved wooden doorway leads into a luminous interior space. The view through the arched entrance reveals a harmonious blend of traditional and contemporary elements, with rustic wood accents and a sleek, modern layout. The soft lighting from above adds a warm, inviting glow.

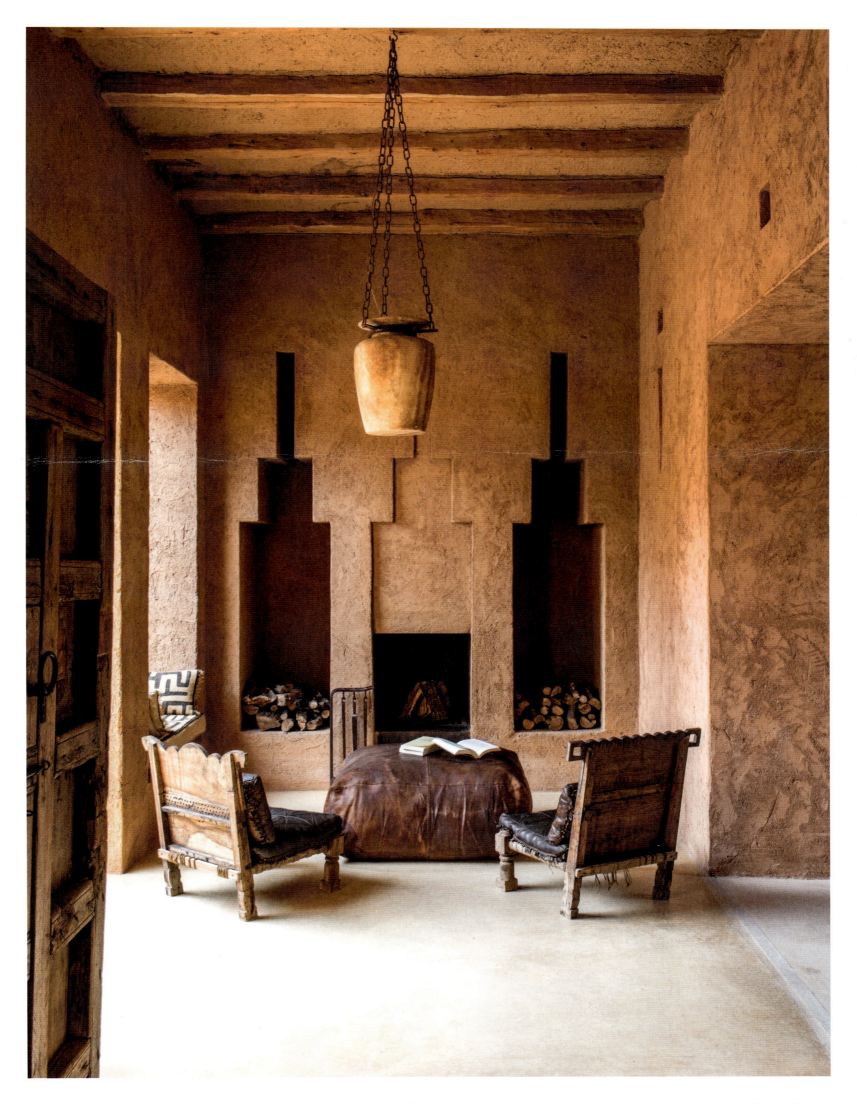

Ochre Oasis

This haven of *tranquility* stands as a testament to the couple's vision, blending *traditional aesthetics* with *contemporary comfort* and preserving the essence of Moroccan craftsmanship

An inviting outdoor dining area features a long, wooden table set under a pergola of natural timber beams. Surrounded by the lush greenery and bathed in natural light, this space embodies the harmony between indoor and outdoor living. The charmingly weathered chairs and the basket of fresh produce add a touch of rustic elegance, making it an ideal setting for gatherings and meals shared in the soothing embrace of nature.

Indian motifs adorn a bedspread atop the bed, near one of the inaugural designs by Studio KO, complemented by a chair discovered in Damascus.

Ochre Oasis

Blending Tradition and Modernity

—·》》 《《·—

This story unfolds with Tessa Sakhi, who embarked on an artistic and creative journey, forging a path marked by beautifully orchestrated imperfection.

Architecture served as the initial common ground, shaping her collective and individual perspective. The establishment of her studio emerged from a desire to reflect on her identity, eschewing a singular focus on discipline in favor of a broader conceptual approach. This philosophy found expression across various mediums, including architecture, urban interventions, public installations, commercial and residential interior design, collectible objects and scenography. Each chosen for its unique expressive potential and capacity to foster interaction. A fascination with imperfection, the narratives carried by materials over time, and the transformative power of accidents and challenges characterizes her work.

A serene living space highlighted by archways and natural light streaming through large doors. The soft green sofas play up comfort and are complemented by greenery and framed art, creating an inviting and harmonious ambiance.

Cutting-edge German speakers by Avantgarde Acoustic pair with 'Saturn' armchairs by Genevieve Dangles and Christian Defrance from 1957, refreshed in Kvadrat fabric, beneath a bespoke chandelier by PSLab. Anchoring the space is a luxurious 3.5m velvet and walnut sofa by Tessa, accompanied by walnut trunk coffee tables that exude natural elegance. Analog travel photos and a Venetian-crafted Murano flask by Tessa enrich the surroundings. An oak desk on glass and a marble and copper coffee table by David/Nicolas seamlessly blend functionality with artistry.

Oriental Living

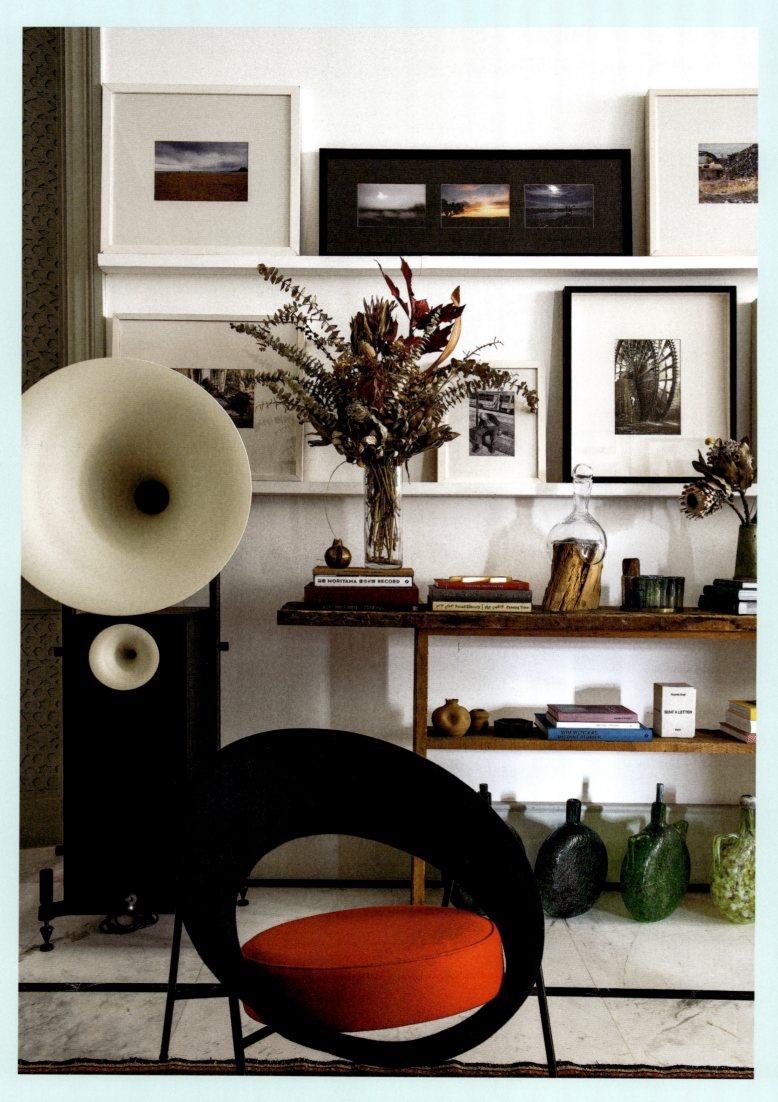

This space is a perfect example of the *harmony* possible between traditional *Lebanese architecture* and an artistic *contemporary* style

The dining room's centerpiece is a custom-designed Burma wood table inspired by Jean Royère's 'Forme Libre' table, surrounded by traditional Lebanese café chairs. Above, a stunning 70-year-old crystal chandelier adds elegance, while a diptych by Lebanese fashion photographer Tarek Moukaddem enhance the room's artistic appeal.

Oriental Living

Setting the tone, a Mondrian-inspired bronze mirror by Tessa is flanked by 'Asset' chairs from David/Nicolas and mid-century chandeliers in rusted brass found in the hidden corners of a flea market in Basta, Lebanon. The room is adorned books by beloved artists and writers, adding layers of inspiration to the space.

> Each piece of bespoke furniture stands as an *artwork*, blending seamlessly into the room's purpose and contributing to the *aesthetic* with materials like *walnut, oak, oxidized brass*, and *patina walls*

The search for a physical space that mirrored her hybrid cultural identity and modern nomadic sensibilities led to the discovery of a house that harmonized traditional Lebanese architecture with contemporary lifestyle needs. Renovated after the 1973 war, this 1930s Lebanese home thoughtfully preserves its traditional character while embracing modern living. The design ethos celebrates Lebanese culture, merging it with contemporary sensibilities through an array of scents, colors, textured materials, traditional arches, cross and barrel vaults, and moucharabieh for softly filtered light. The house is bifurcated into two distinct sections: the living and common areas, designed for social gatherings with family, friends, colleagues, and clients; and the private quarters, dedicated to bedrooms and personal spaces.

Each piece of furniture is bespoke, meticulously tailored to its environment. These pieces stand as artworks, subtly embodying the room's purpose. In communal areas, light wireframe designs subtly blend into the space, while intimate areas are adorned with furniture in warm hues. The design maximizes natural light, employing a warm color palette that layers rich textures and shades. Materials such as walnut and oak wood, oxidized brass and copper, patina walls, and large wooden window arches contribute to the aesthetic. Floors in communal spaces feature Italian Calacatta and Nero Marquina marble, contrasting with the private areas, which boast reclaimed traditional ceramic tiles from old Lebanese homes, set against wood, melding heritage with contemporary design.

The office space showcases a Herman Miller Eames rocking chair by Vitra and a 'Polygon' armchair by Prostoria. A custom-designed desk made from oak wood mounted on thick glass adds a touch of artisanal craftsmanship. Black metal shelves with copper screws hold architecture books and files, providing both functionality and style.

A cozy corner featuring a soft green sofa beneath a gallery wall of eclectic framed art. Natural light streams through large arched windows, illuminating the space and highlighting the mix of textures and patterns.

> Tessa Sakhi has not only redefined the *concept of space* but also illustrated the *profound* connection between *heritage* and *innovation*

A central gallery space bridges the communal and private realms of the house, facilitating a fluid visual and physical connection. This area, dedicated to communal activities, is enriched with greenery and art, leading to individually themed rooms designed to cater to varying moods and needs, demonstrating a commitment to blending tradition with contemporary expressions of culture.

In crafting a narrative that transcends the boundaries of traditional design, Tessa Sakhi has not only redefined the concept of space but also illustrated the profound connection between heritage and innovation. Her journey, one of discovery, collaboration, and creation, serves as a beacon for aspiring designers and architects. It underscores the importance of embracing one's roots while simultaneously pushing the envelope of creativity. Her work, a testament to the power of shared vision and mutual respect, stands as an inspiring example of how diverse backgrounds and perspectives can come together to forge not just spaces, but stories that resonate with a wide array of audiences. —

The breakfast room features a 'Fraqué' wood table by Tessa, showcasing 1848 Louis-Philippe Sèvres porcelain alongside a global collection of crystals and ceramics, illuminated by Davide Groppi 'Miss' pendants. The vibrant red walls add a pop of color and warmth to the space.

(right) In the adjoining kitchen, all-white cabinetry and Corian countertops provide a sleek, contemporary look, while the geometric patterned floor tiles add a touch of classic elegance. A large, black pendant light hangs from the high ceiling, creating a bold focal point. The vibrant red pantry in the background adds a pop of color and warmth to the space.

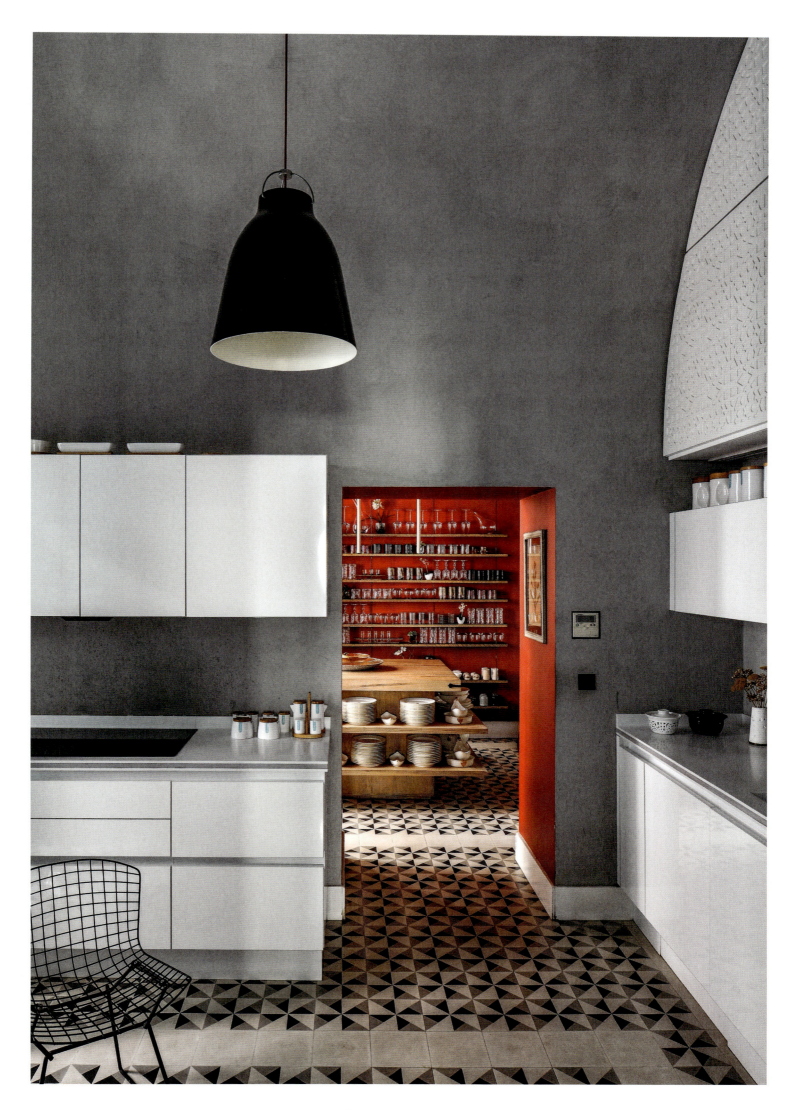

Blending Tradition and Modernity

The master bedroom, set against a backdrop of cross-vaults and traditional ceramic tiles mixed with wood, features Flos and Catellani & Smith lighting. A Tessa walnut canopy bed, highlighted by a Moooi 'Random' Pendant, becomes the room's focal point, merging timeless design with modern aesthetics.

The Happy Farm in the Valley

—·⟩⟩⟨⟨·—

A farm that mirrors the vibrant hues of the Bekaa sets the stage for a narrative of tradition, innovation, and celebration. Through the evolution of its architecture, Issa farm embodies the fusion of Lebanese heritage with the warmth of familial hospitality.

Constructed in 1969, Issa Farm is shaped like a U, with three rectangular sections surrounding a cool water basin, two of which feature an additional story. The exterior, dyed to match the golden wheat of Bekaa, has witnessed numerous transformations yet remains deeply rooted in its origins. Its flat roof and thick walls stand resilient against the valley's dramatic temperature swings, ensuring comfort amidst the extremes.

This charming archway, adorned with rustic wooden doors and vitange green benches, invites visitors into the heart of the Bekaa Valley home, where history and warmth converge.

A farm that mirrors the *vibrant hues* of the Bekaa *sets the stage*, evolving with each generation while rooted in its origins

This inviting living area, with its warm old rose walls, traditional cushions, and central fireplace, embodies the essence of Lebanese hospitality and timeless charm.

Oriental Living

The entryway, with its traditional arch and intricate latticework, sets a welcoming tone. A carved wooden sideboard adorned with decorative items enhances the space's cultural richness. Arak, the traditional Lebanese drink, is served on a wooden tray to accompany a varied mezze. The etched brass oriental coffee table features beautifully designed wooden boxes and serving dishes, perfect for gathering and sharing stories.

The foundation is a simple rectangle, serving as the initial building block. As time passes, the structure evolves with the ebb and flow of family generations and the changing seasons. With each passing year, new sections are seamlessly added. As the family expands, another rectangle joins the first, followed by a third that draws inspiration from Andalusian haciendas, while the fourth encloses an inner courtyard (*dar*). Covered walkways (*iwan*) connect different areas, and extended roofs supported by wooden colonnades (*rwak*) offer protection from the rain.

> **Traditional design elements like *wall niches*, built-in pantries, and *shelves* blend function with *cultural heritage*, adorned with *regional artifacts* and antiques**

Traditional design elements like wall niches (*yuk*) for storage, built-in pantries (*namlieh*), and shelves (*rfouf*) blend function with cultural heritage, and are adorned with myriad decorative plates, mirrors, and handcrafted clay sculptures. The interior spaces, centered around cozy fireplaces, are adorned with regional artifacts and antiques from across Lebanon, including the oud, large oil jars, intricately carved chairs, and vintage doors, celebrating the area's rich history.

In 2001, an upstairs apartment featuring a modern kitchen, library, cozy living room, and several bedrooms was introduced, offering warmth and convenience during the cold winter months, just an hour and twenty minutes from the capital, making it an inviting retreat for the family.

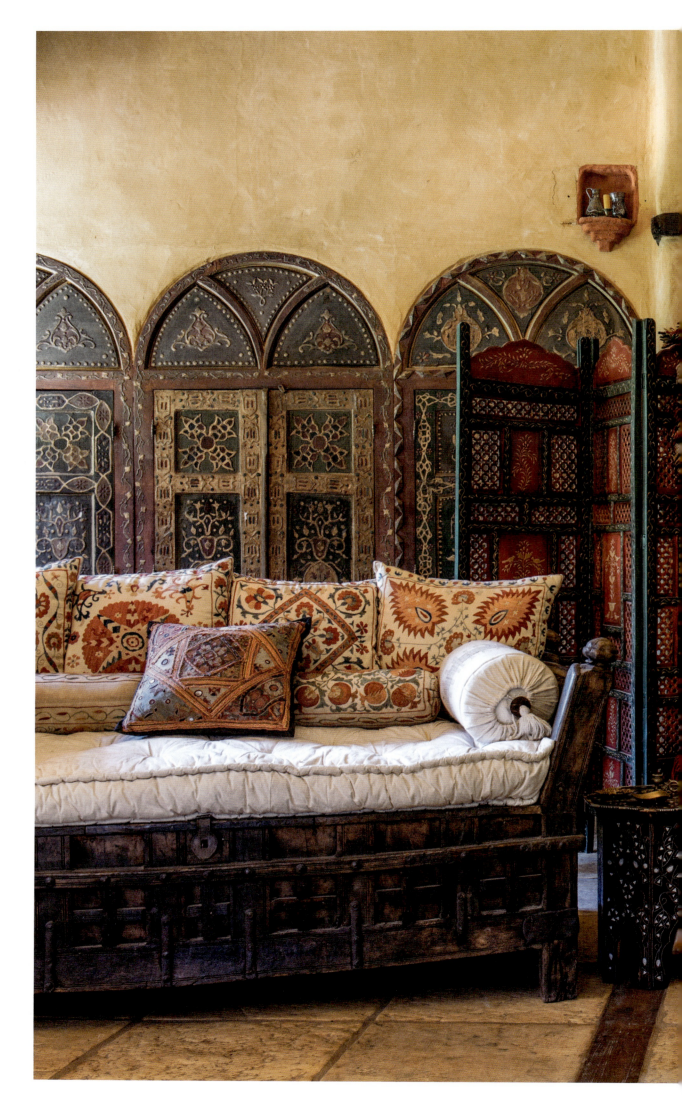

An array of intricately painted doors and circular wicker mats, alongside carved wooden screens and ornate cushions, weave together tales of Lebanon's rich history.

Oriental Living

The Happy Farm in the Valley

The Happy Farm in the Valley

This beautifully designed bathroom features traditional earthen sinks, round mirrors, and warm wooden beams, blending practicality with cultural charm. Colorful baskets and vintage fixtures add to the inviting, timeless atmosphere.

Karm el Joz, nestled among *walnut groves*, offers a *serene setting* for celebrations, blending *natural beauty* with a sense of peace and enduring *happiness*

The farm is alive with horses, donkeys, sheep, and other animals, with a honey-colored kitten accompanying visitors, reflecting the hospitality of the locals. The warmth of our hosts, Claude Issa and her daughter Audrey, rivals the brightness of the sun that nurtures the countless trees they lovingly plant. Responding to the growing demand for a picturesque venue, the Issa sisters inaugurated a separate facility in 2016, designed for celebrations amid the walnut groves. This space, Karm el Joz, stands as a testament to exclusive happiness, nestled among diverse tree species and hundreds of walnut trees near Issa farm. It began hosting weddings within months of its conception, and offers a serene backdrop with a cozy lounge, kitchen, bedrooms, and terraces overlooking the greenery.

An outdoor kitchen caters to event needs, allowing clients to personalize their celebrations while respecting the natural setting with predefined lighting and sound requirements. The venue, capable of hosting up to 1,200 seated guests, champions customization, making each event uniquely memorable. Audrey Issa, now overseeing Karm el Joz events, speaks of the palpable, enduring happiness that defines the venue. —

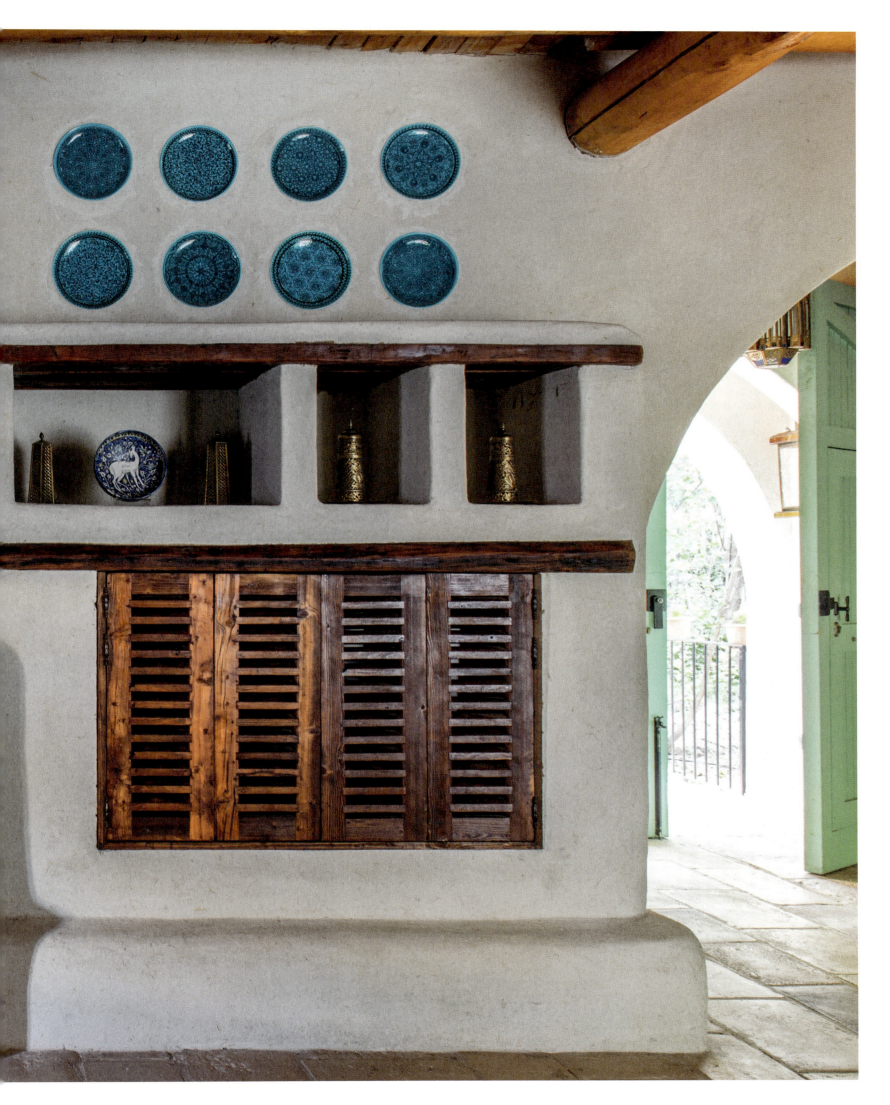

This outdoor space invites guests to sit and enjoy the natural surroundings. The leafy canopy and wooden beams create a peaceful retreat for relaxation and contemplation, blending seamlessly with the lush greenery.

A Thousand and One Nights

—·»〉〈«·—

Zeina Aboukheir has masterfully converted a dilapidated 1940s residence into a masterpiece reminiscent of an Orientalist artwork. Nestled in the heart of Beirut's Mar Mikhael district, this dwelling has undergone extensive restoration. It is now adorned with wall frescoes and decorated with an eclectic array of 1950s furniture sourced from around the globe.

Upon entry, guests are immediately captivated by the heritage ceiling lights reminiscent of ancient Baghdad homes and unique light fixtures from Basta. The living room is anchored by a contemporary couch upholstered in damascene purple velvet, traditionally used in bridal dowries, beneath an expansive 18th-century Russian painting. Accentuating the space are a large sofa and British mosaic tables atop a Karabakh Kilim rug. Illuminating the dining area is an Italian chandelier adorned with colorful Murano glass fruits, surrounded by sleek chairs.

A vibrant blend of cultural influences, this room in Zeina Aboukheir's Mar Mikhael residence showcases intricate Syrian inlay furniture, vivid 1950s armchairs, and a dynamic modern painting, capturing the essence of a timeless Oriental elegance.

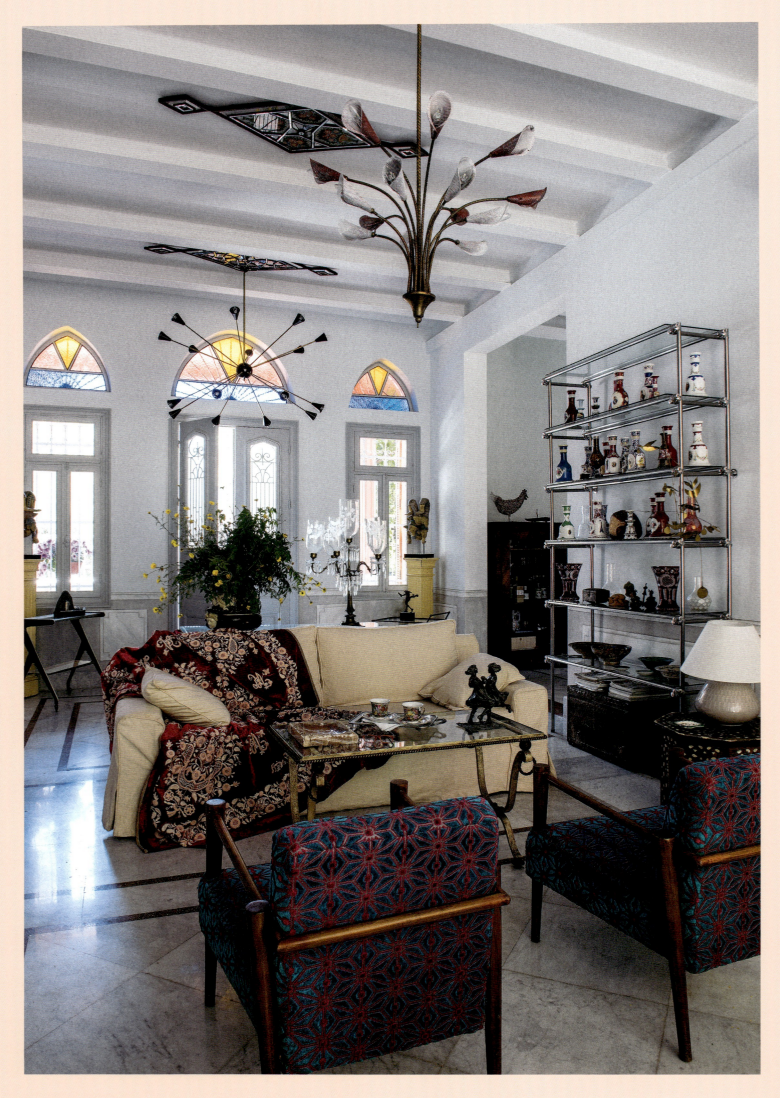

Oriental Living

Upon entering, you are welcomed into a living room illuminated by chandeliers from the 1950s, acquired from Basta, the antiques district in Beirut. A contemporary white sofa, adorned with purple damascene velvet featuring intricate embroidery, faces a pair of armchairs from the same era.

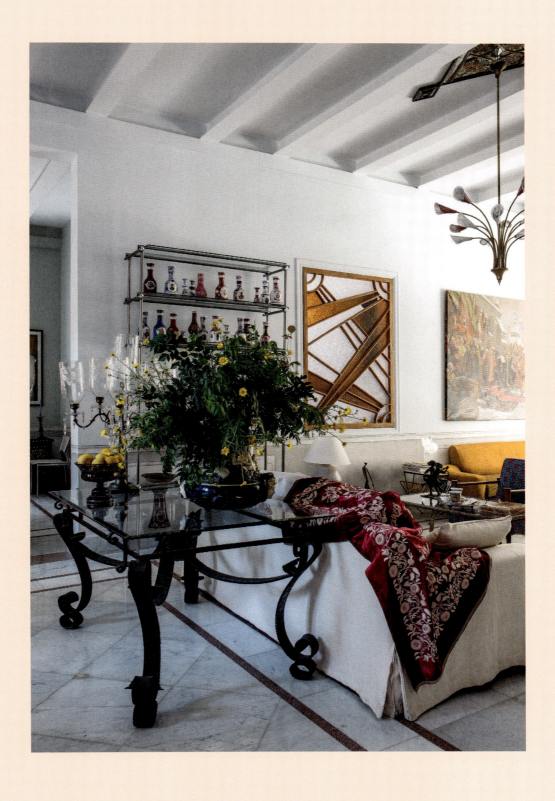

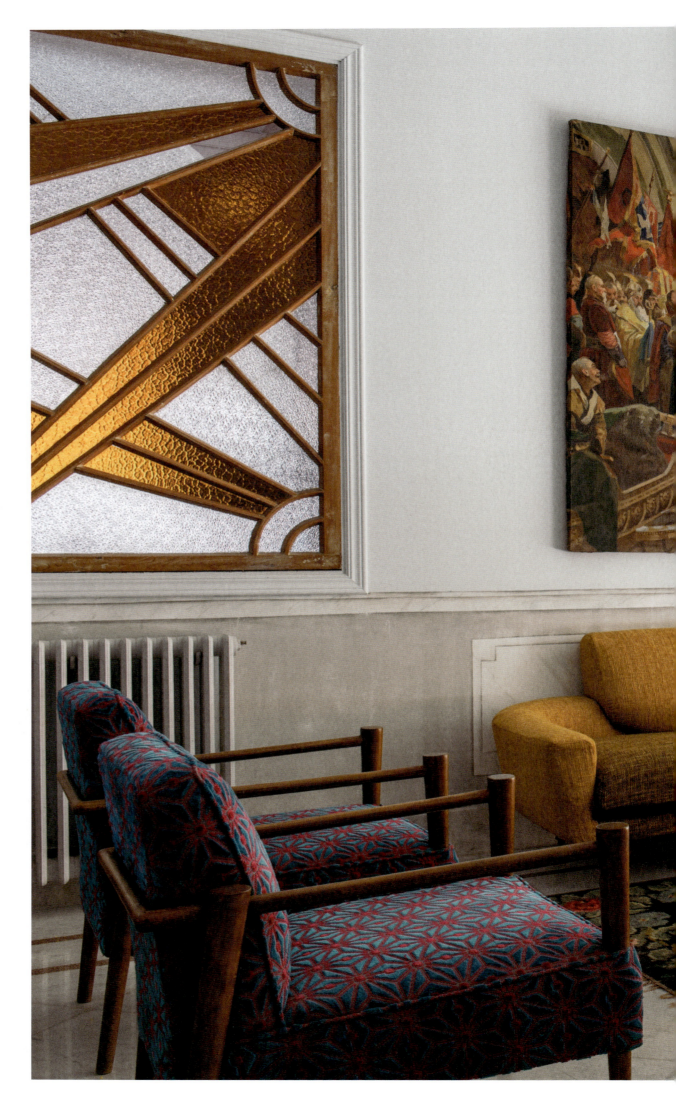

A sofa and armchairs from the 1950s are overshadowed by a grand 18th-century Russian painting depicting the Tsar reading an ukase. Below, a Karabagh kilim adorns the floor.

Oriental Living

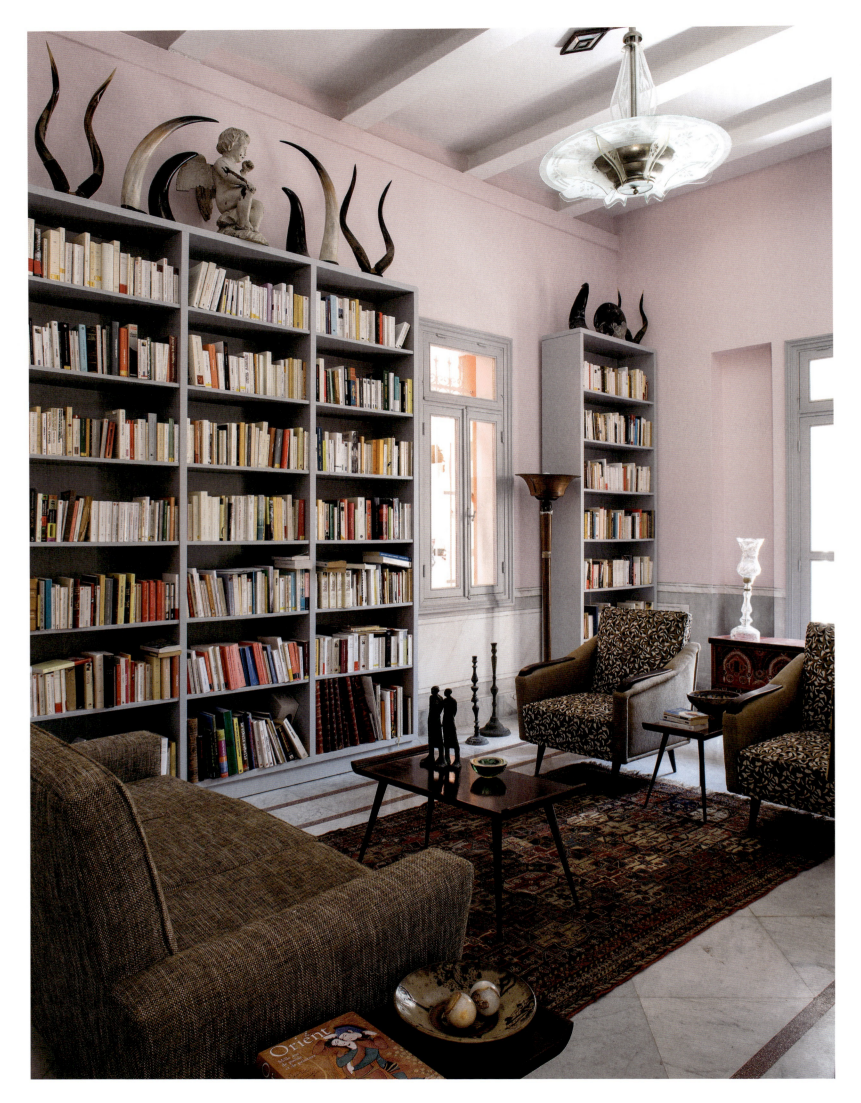

In this cozy reading room, towering bookshelves filled with literary treasures are complemented by plush armchairs and a vintage sofa, creating a serene oasis for relaxation. The room's soft pink walls and antique decor, including a Persian rug and unique sculptures, add a touch of refined elegance and cultural depth.

> Every corner of Beit Zanzoun *tells a story*, from the carefully selected *antique furnishings* to the art that adorns its walls, offering guests an *immersive* experience

Iraqi craftsmanship shines through with colored Baghdad glass ceiling lights adding to the ambiance. Two modern paintings adorn the walls above Damascus-style chests inlaid with mother-of-pearl, creating an unmistakable Orientalist vibe. Zeina, a photographer and jewelry designer with a penchant for Oriental culture, possesses a keen eye for unearthing treasures in various souks.

The pathway to the bedrooms is marked by a refreshing vibrant blue hue, complemented by the gleam of a gold leaf-adorned lift shaft and wrought-iron railing.

The upstairs greets guests with a serene angel perched in a Sabil, a traditional public marble fountain. A Biedermeier sofa from Austria, draped in pink Egyptian cotton, enhances the tranquility of the space. The azure walls are adorned with a 19th-century Cairo painting and a Moroccan chandelier from Rabat dangles above.

The bedrooms enchant with copper beds imported from Alexandria, dressed in Suzani fabrics from Uzbekistan, and Damascus-style furniture embellished with mother-of-pearl. Art-deco light fixtures and Cairo cotton curtains featuring Arabic calligraphy complete the decor. In Zeina's bedroom, a magnificent mural by Lebanese artist Mario Dahabi serves as the headboard, while floral designs by Dahabi adorn the bathroom, leaving his artistic mark throughout the home.

This staircase, leading to the second-floor bedrooms, showcases a harmonious blend of blue and gold. The wrought-iron handrail is adorned with gold leaf, adding an elegant touch.

Zeina Aboukheir has masterfully *converted* a 1940s home in Beirut's Mar Mikhael district into a *masterpiece* reminiscent of an *Orientalist artwork*

Departing from Beit Zanzoun, as this guest house is named, guests carry with them visions of exotic tales, eager to return and experience a stay, if only for a night, and to savour a coffee on the charming ancient terrace that wraps around the property.

This unique abode not only offers a visual journey through the Orient but also encapsulates the essence of cultural fusion and historical preservation. Zeina's vision has breathed new life into this historical structure, blending traditional elements with contemporary design to pays homage to the rich tapestry of Eastern cultures. Every corner of Beit Zanzoun narrates a story, from the carefully selected antique furnishings to the art that adorns its walls, providing guests with an immersive experience that transcends mere accommodation. It stands as a testament to the beauty of restoration, the art of interior design, and the power of bringing diverse cultural artifacts together under one roof, creating a sanctuary that not only preserves memories of the past but also inspires dreams for the future. —

A modern dining table is lit by an Italian chandelier crafted from multicolored Murano glass. The ceiling lights, sourced from Baghdad, complement the setting, and at the room's far end, above two chests inlaid with damascene mother-of-pearl, hang two modern paintings.

This unique abode serves as a *visual journey* through the Orient, embodying *cultural fusion* and *historical preservation* in a way that pays homage to Eastern cultures

In this anteroom, an Austrian Biedermeier sofa, upholstered in fuchsia Suzani fabric, is paired with a Karabagh rug.

A Thousand and One Nights

Oriental Living

The copper canopy bed, sourced from Alexandria, Egypt, is adorned with a Suzani bedspread from Uzbekistan. The curtains, featuring Arabic calligraphy embroidery, were sourced in Cairo.

(below) An exquisite glass bottle featuring a Madonna and Child stands beside a vintage candelabrum, set against a backdrop of intricate Arabic calligraphy, blending spiritual symbolism with artistic elegance.

(right) In one of the bedrooms, an antique copper bed covered in Suzani fabric is paired with 1950s armchairs and art-deco lighting.

Oriental Living

(left) An artwork by Mario Dahabi serves as a divider between the bedroom and the bathroom.

(right) Damascene wood and mother-of-pearl cabinet featuring a gilded wood angel.

Beit Zanzoun, with its copper beds, mother-of-pearl inlaid furniture, and *stunning murals*, provides guests with a stay that feels like stepping into a *living work* of art

The bathroom in Beit Zanzoun is adorned with *intricate floral murals* blending art and functionality in a truly *unique* way

This vibrant bathroom, featuring a floral mural by Mario Dahabi, combines luxurious details with artistic charm. The ornate mirrors and white marble countertops add a touch of elegance, while the gold-accented walls and colorful furnishings create a harmonious and inviting space.

The Governor's Palace

—·»}{«·—

In the heart of Byblos, Lebanon, a city renowned as the oldest continuously inhabited metropolis in the world, stands the Governor's Palace, an architectural relic from the Ottoman Empire. The palace was brought back to life by the meticulous by Joseph Achkar and Michel Charrière. The duo embarked on a delicate mission not to renovate but to preserve, offering visitors a seamless journey through time.

This room highlights the ornate beauty of antique furniture, featuring intricately carved wooden chairs and an elegant table set with fine crystal and silverware. The centerpiece, a stunning Murano glass chandelier, hangs majestically from the ceiling, adding a touch of opulence. The beautifully preserved architectural details, including arched windows and doors with intricate woodwork, evoke a sense of timeless elegance and grandeur, reflecting the rich history and refined taste of its owners.

Spanning over 7,000 years of civilisation, Byblos is a testament to the enduring human spirit. Perched amidst the mountains and overlooking the ancient Phoenician port, the Governor's Palace served as its administrative hub during the Ottoman rule. Discovered by Achkar and Charrière in a remarkable state of preservation, the palace's interior is a time capsule of authenticity. They undertook a restoration that pays homage to the historical essence. The ancient paintings gracing the walls and ceilings silently narrate tales from bygone eras, while the preserved floors and spatial layouts retain their authentic historical character.

A trio of traditional arched windows light up an open-plan, cross-shaped central hall. At its heart is a marble basin inviting thoughts of serenity, while its walls and ceilings are still covered in the original 18th-century frescoes.

The Governor's Palace

Ottoman abayas recount the journeys of the Silk Road.

Oriental Living

The Governor's Palace

The palace's architecture, a classical testament to its era, has been faithfully preserved. The ground floor, once the heartbeat of daily chores, houses the kitchen, laundry and servants' quarters. Ascending to the first floor reveals the grandeur of reception areas and master bedrooms. A secretive top floor, historically the domain of women, completes the architectural narrative. In an age devoid of a formal architectural profession in Lebanon, builders masterfully crafted living spaces that resonated with the natural landscape, materials and light. This palace, a product of such ingenuity, exudes tranquillity, serenity, and a unique charm that shifts with the sun's dance across the sky.

Each room in the palace tells its own story, as Achkar describes, with some inviting relaxation and introspection, while others, adorned with an array of objects and a distinctive moucharabieh, offer a different ambiance, perhaps tinged with a subtle sense of intrigue.

The restoration extended thoughtfully to the bathroom, where modernity and tradition converge. Natural light filters through glass cabochons, reminiscent of ancient hammams, while a Damascus basin, now equipped with contemporary amenities, anchors the space. Even the stone basins, sourced from Istanbul's souks and holding Aleppo soaps, contribute to the narrative, whispering tales of the region's rich trading history.

The former audience chamber features turquoise walls, long Ottoman-style sofas and stunning wooden-framed windows with bird details.

Each piece of furniture is bespoke, *meticulously tailored* to its environment

Intriguingly, the absence of a dining room in the palace sparks curiosity, to which Joseph responds with historical context, noting the late emergence of such a space in Middle Eastern architecture. Instead, dining was a versatile affair, with the setting dictated by the day's mood, light, and company, ranging from a room to the garden.

Years of restoration have not altered the essence of the Governor's Palace but rather enhanced its narrative. For Michel, the integrity of an ancient abode is akin to poetry, where altering a single line can disrupt the entire harmony. Joseph, reflecting on the project, sees it not as vanity but as a vessel for life's pivotal moments. In the Governor's Palace, every corner, every stone and every beam narrate a story, preserved and cherished through time. —

(left) The blue walls are adorned with framed artwork and antique plates, while the wooden ceiling beams add a rustic charm. An ornate brass lantern hangs, illuminating the room's rich tapestry of colors and textures.

(above) A beautifully arranged table adorned with crystal glassware, ornate silverware, and antique furnishings, including a stunning blue vase and intricately carved wooden pieces. Adding a lively contrast to the meticulously detailed interior, a colorful macaw perches elegantly on an antique stand.

(left) The governor's chamber, on the main level, is furnished with an elaborate canopy bed , brought back from India.

(below) The soft blue and green walls, adorned with delicate patterns, complement the chest's vintage charm. On top of the chest, a framed vintage photo and a decorative box add to the room's historical ambiance.

(next page) the opulent bedrooms are accessed through the central hall and feature stunning inlaid furniture.

The Governor's Palace

Oriental Living

An array of treasures, including framed miniature portraits, a beautifully carved chair with intricate mother-of-pearl inlay work, and various antique findings. Together, they reflect the palace's blend of historical elegance and opulent design, showcasing a space where every detail tells a story of grandeur and refinement.

(next page) Modernity and tradition converge in the bathroom. Natural light filters through glass cabochons onto a large Damascus basin.

Pink Palm Grove

—·›〉〈‹·—

Within the serene pink palm oasis of Marrakech, a couple enamored with Morocco's tranquil off-season atmosphere enlisted the expertise of Pinto studio to create their ideal home. They envisioned a space filled with vibrant colors and exquisite treasures.

As avid collectors of contemporary art from the 1950s and 1960s, as well as passionate antique seekers and world travelers, the homeowners embrace boldness. Their eclectic taste combines fine art and local market finds, daringly mixing unconventional decor, a thirst for vibrant colors, and warmth without hesitation. To elevate their home for gatherings with friends from London and beyond, they once again turned to the talents of Alberto Pinto's studio, along with Pietro Scaglione, a trusted project manager from the Parisian firm. Tasked with expanding and redesigning a home originally crafted by architect Charles Boccara within Marrakech's palm groves, the project spanned two years and covered 3,000 square meters, including a dozen bedrooms and a sprawling three-hectare garden.

The ground-floor corridor dazzles in hues of red and gold, extending the living room's theme with matching Pena carpets and curtains. Decorative pieces include a Talmaris Plinth and chandeliers sourced from souks.

Anchored by a custom Pena carpet designed by Pinto, the ground-floor living room is furnished with vintage pieces, chairs dressed in Pierre Frey Shanghai fabric, and 'Noles' sofas upholstered in Pierre Frey chenille fabric in Braise red.

Pink Palm Grove

(below) An ornate alcove window is framed with red floral friezes.

(right) The upper-level living room showcases chairs that harmonize with the turquoise zellige of the fireplace and features carpet designs by Pietro Scaglione for Pinto.

The brief was clear and ambitious: to create a home that stands out with its unique blend of eclectic design, boldness, and exclusivity, ensuring a warm, inviting atmosphere for guests. The design unfolds through a series of spaces, ranging from vast open areas like a covered terrace to more secluded spots such as the lady's boudoir and the children's bedrooms. This design strategy leads to a delightful clash of styles, where an English painting from the 1950s, an ancient Oriental kiosk, a zellige-tiled fireplace, and Berber-patterned carpets – all reimagined by Pietro Scaglione – coexist. The Pinto studio, known for its exceptional use of materials, craftsmanship, and meticulous attention to detail, attracts clients with distinctive tastes. These clients are deeply involved in the design process, supported by frequent consultations, to bring their vision of a dream home to life, elevated to its fullest expression.

This Marrakech retreat stands as a testament to the harmonious blend of diverse cultures and artistic expressions, underpinned by the guiding vision of the Alberto Pinto studio. Each space within the house tells a story of discovery, blending the rich heritage of Moroccan craftsmanship with the refined aesthetics of contemporary and antique collections from around the globe. The result is a living masterpiece that not only serves as a sanctuary for its inhabitants but also as an inspiring gathering place that reflects the adventurous spirits of its owners. Through this project, the boundaries of traditional design are expanded, illustrating how personal vision, when executed with expert guidance, can transform a space into an extraordinary experience.
—

(previous page) In the dining room, a mural by local decorators Engebo sets a backdrop for a space adorned with a chandelier, wall lights, and a monkey console by Tzumindi, invoking the wild charm of the 'Planet of the Apes.'

(right) An Alberto Pinto-designed headboard crafted by Scènes d'intérieur (Rabat), paired with Shanghai Pierre Frey fabric and leather accents. A BD Design Snake Light and vintage architectural drawings add a touch of sophistication.

> This Marrakech retreat stands as a testament to the *harmonious blend* of diverse cultures and *artistic expressions*, underpinned by the guiding vision of the Alberto Pinto studio

Pink Palm Grove

A guestroom adorned with a vintage Suzani bedspread and 1950s chairs, creating a warm and nostalgic atmosphere.

Oriental Living

(left) This sophisticated bathroom, with a vaulted brick ceiling and an alabaster pendant light, features a regal blue and gold chair at a stylish coiffeuse.

(above) Vibrant botanical prints and striking blue and green vases infuse color and charm. A trio of beaded African masks adds a touch of global sophistication, reflecting an appreciation for diverse cultures and artistic expression.

The *design* unfolds through a series of spaces, ranging from vast *open areas* to more *secluded spots*, creating a delightful clash of styles and *vibrant* colors

(left) A Tataoui ceiling, masterfully painted by Engebo, oversees a space illuminated by a Blaoui Marrakech chandelier and centered around a Fantoni 'Piazza' sculpture. 'Embassy' sofas and chairs by Boncina are draped in fabrics from Duralee Pavilion and Holland & Sherry, atop a custom carpet inspired by Calder de Molina's work.

(below) Vintage seating, revived with Vano and Sanderson fabrics, creates a cosy boudoir and dressing area, gently illuminated by charming heart-shaped lampshades.

The homeowners eclectic taste combines *fine art* and *local market finds*, daringly mixing unconventional decor, a thirst for *vibrant* colors, and *warmth* without hesitation

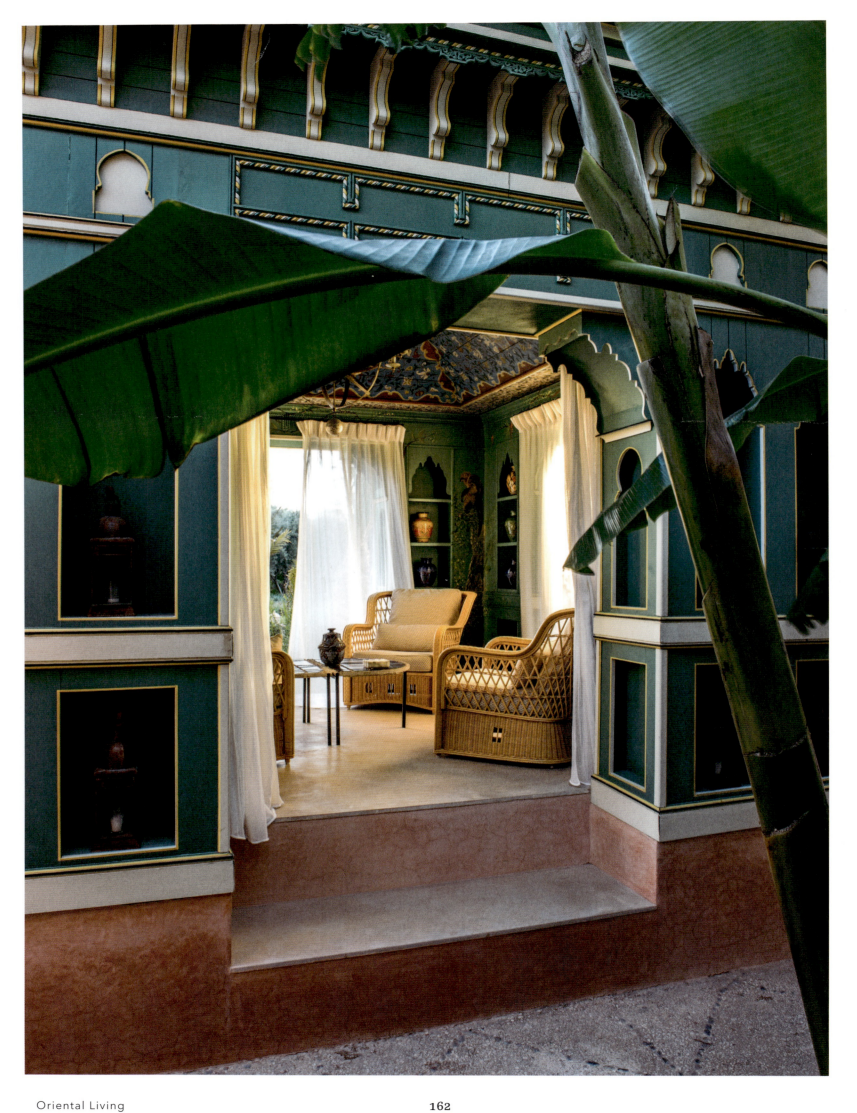

The garden room's retro coffee table is complemented by Engebo's decorative art., 'Crochet' seating by Bonacina with textiles by Duralee Pavilion and Holland & Sherry by Champalimaud Design. Souk-sourced vases add a touch of local flair.

(next page) The outdoor dining area is housed in a painted wooden pavilion with voile curtains. Inside, a lively color palette of green, red, gold, and more, enlivens the space with dynamic energy.

Pink Palm Grove

Bohemian Chic

—⋅⇢⇠⋅—

Tucked away in a courtyard in Gemmayzé, an authentic Beirut neighborhood, lies a secluded mansion, over a century old. Here, Maria Hibri has masterfully crafted an ambiance where hues and textures blend effortlessly, invoking both harmony and whimsy. This enchanting setting captivates the imagination, showcasing a décor that champions the power of creative thought.

Maria Hibri shines as an extraordinary interior designer, renowned for her visionary approach. Alongside the multi-talented artist Hoda Baroudi, she co-founded Bokja, a trailblazing brand celebrated for its daring innovation. Their creations, especially the armchairs embellished with a vibrant blend of embroidery and vintage fabrics, have garnered global recognition, epitomising the forefront of contemporary Oriental design. The skillful art of blending textures, forms and colors, revitalising vintage furniture, refurbishing floors, and highlighting historical architectural elements reflects a remarkable talent. This process often mirrors the creative journey of an artist, whether in painting, fashion design, or poetry, manifesting here in the curation of exquisite living spaces.

(next page) The interiors are full of unexpected combinations: a 'Seven Stages of the Heart' armchair by Bokja sits opposite a statue of the Virgin Mary painted in fluorescent pink.

(right) A vibrant showcase of eclectic elegance, this living room combines rich colors, textures, and artistic elements. The striking yellow chandelier and curated artwork complement the mix of modern and vintage furniture.

(below) Upholstered in vintage fabric, this armchair is a collaboration between Bokja and Wissem Nochi. A mosaic table with sundried apricots and a cup of tea create an inviting corner within the home.

Bohemian Chic

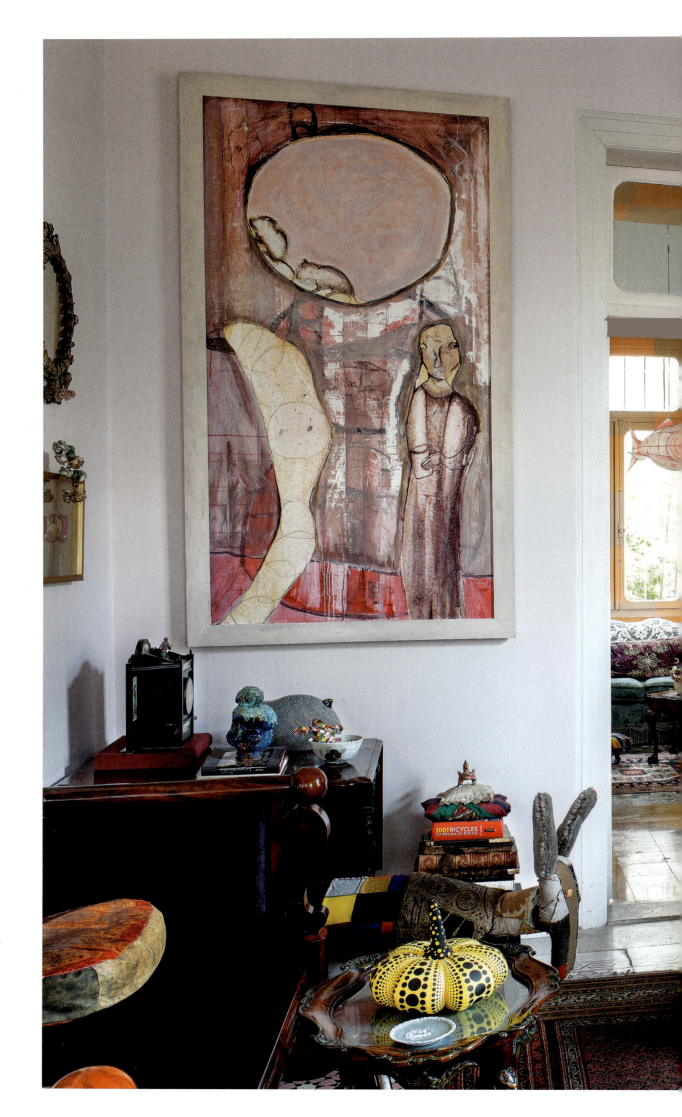

The turquoise armchair paired with a patterned ottoman, alongside the rich textures of the Bokja cushions, adds a touch of comfort and sophistication. The juxtaposition of contemporary and traditional elements makes this space a true testament to Maria Hibri's creative vision.

Oriental Living

Bohemian Chic

Hibri's approach to redesigning the space is marked by the layering of various elements without strict adherence to a specific style, embracing the courage to blend disparate items. Among these eclectic elements stands a striking fuchsia pink Virgin Mary statue facing a yellow armchair from Basta, alongside a chair from Bokja's 'Seven Stages of the Heart' series, a venture exploring Sufism with designer Wyssem Nochi. The décor is further enriched with Karabagh floral carpets underfoot and walls painted in Caribbean blue, adorned with an equestrian photograph by Hibri's daughter Ayla, and artworks by Marwan Sahmarani and Zeina el-Khalil.

The living room presents another spectacle of vibrant colors, featuring a Syrian yellow chandelier, a Malayer rug, a blue armchair from Basta, and a Bokja pouf. The dining area further exemplifies the art of juxtaposition with a Piet Hein Eek table surrounded by an eclectic mix of chairs, an Aubusson tapestry, and a Saint-Louis chandelier, creating a captivating ensemble.

Visitors are left in awe, their senses invigorated by this poetic space where each object is thoughtfully placed, akin to the deliberate arrangement of words in a poem.

Venturing through Maria Hibri's creation feels like a journey across time and space, where each corner reveals a story and every artifact whispers tales of distant lands. This haven is not just a testament to Hibri's impeccable taste but also a tribute to the art of storytelling through design. It's a space where the past and present converge, inviting guests to lose themselves in a visual narrative that defies convention. Hibri's ability to orchestrate this symphony of colors, textures and historical elements transforms the mansion into a living canvas, celebrating the beauty of diversity and the endless possibilities of imagination. This enchanting environment serves as a vivid reminder of how spaces can evoke emotions, stimulate creativity, and foster a deep appreciation for the intricate tapestry of global cultures. —

(previous page) Green and orange blend gracefully here, despite the contradiction between the modern, checkerboard wallpaper designed by Annabel Kassar and the Rococo armchair.

(right) Under a Saint-Louis crystal chandelier is a Piet Hein Eek table found at Rossana Orlandi in Milan and surrounded by a series of chairs by Bokja.

> In this *poetic space*, each object is thoughtfully placed, akin to the deliberate arrangement of words in a *poem*, creating a captivating *visual narrative*

Bohemian Chic

The house is surrounded by a lush garden adorned with palm trees. A serene balcony with intricate, wrought-iron furniture creates an idyllic spot for relaxation. The vintage table, set with colorful glassware, and the vibrant floral-patterned chair invite you to unwind and enjoy the tranquil surroundings.

The Gem of Marrakech

—·»‹‹·—

At the center of Marrakech lies a timeless treasure, La Mamounia. This landmark luxury hotel embodies a philosophy of sophistication and grace. With each passing year and through every thoughtful renovation, this iconic establishment has beautifully preserved its allure, always presenting itself anew.

Nestled within lush gardens, La Mamounia paints a vivid picture of Marrakech, showcasing its ochre hues in every season. Under the sun's radiant warmth, which seems to shine brighter here than anywhere else, a vibrant tapestry of giant cacti, radiant rosebushes, and ancient olive, orange, mandarin and palm trees unfolds. Amidst this natural splendour, contrasts of shadow and light create a captivating play, wild thickets and orderly avenues offer a peaceful retreat, allowing you to drift away from the hustle and bustle of the nearby souks and the vibrant Jemaa el-Fnaa square, into a serene symphony of birdsong. The estate is dotted with pools and fountains, their waters dancing in the magical light. La Mamounia, though a century old, remains as timeless as ever.

Nestled within the lush gardens of La Mamounia, this picturesque scene showcases the intricate mosaic pillars adorned with vibrant geometric patterns, a testament to the exquisite Moroccan craftsmanship. The serene ambiance is further enhanced by the surrounding greenery and the dappled sunlight, creating a tranquil retreat.

A garden where wild beauty gently unfolds its tales. A lantern-lined path leads from the hotel's Churchill Bar to its main entrance.

Oriental Living

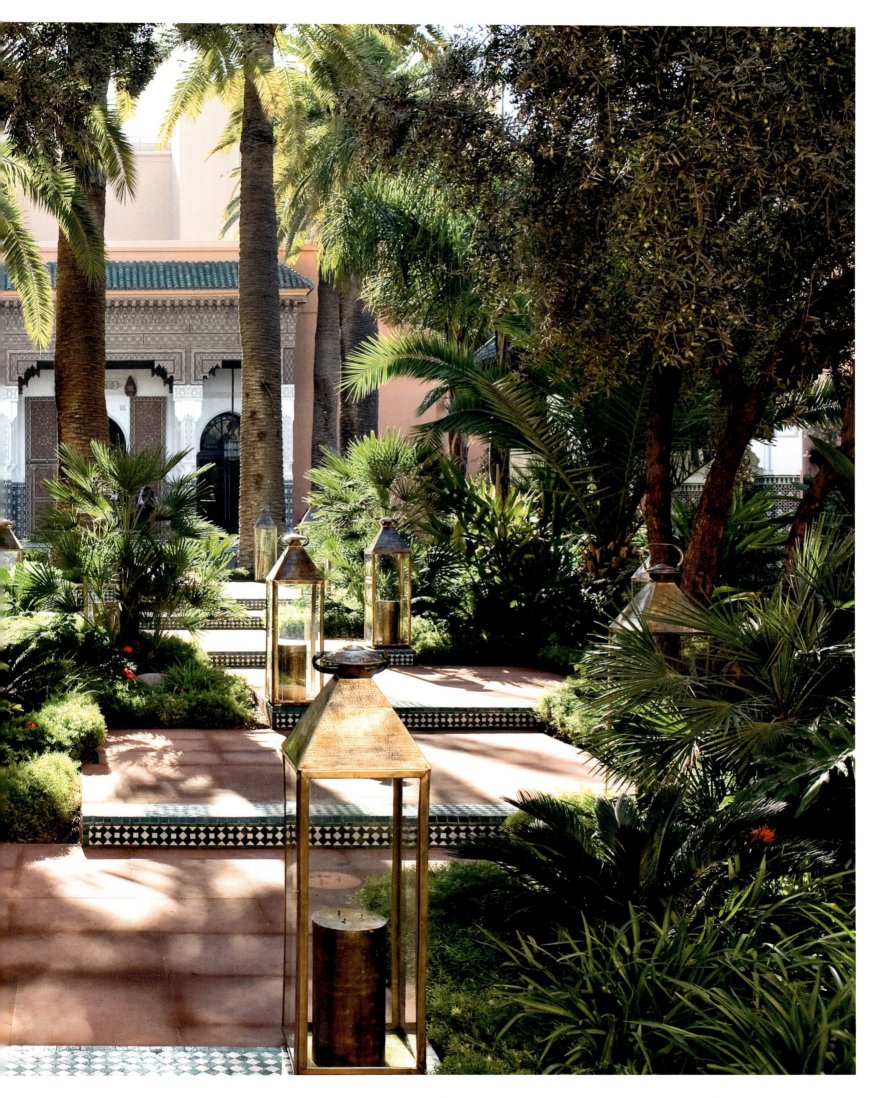

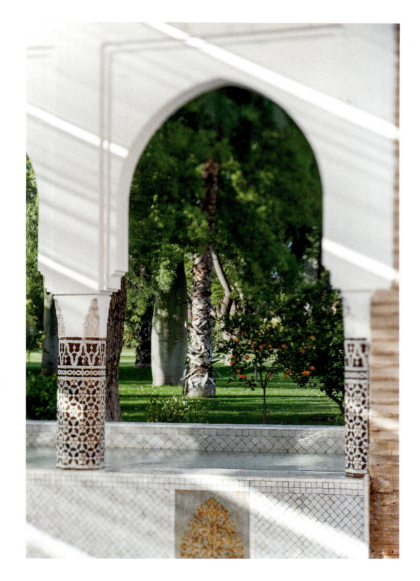

(above) With 27 fountains and basins, the flow of water marks the rhythm of the surroundings and moments within.

(left) In the Moroccan restaurant, rich textures and ornate details create an atmosphere of regal splendor. A plush velvet chair invites relaxation, while a nearby table, set with fine glassware and plates, hints at the exquisite dining experience to come. This scene perfectly encapsulates the luxurious blend of Moroccan artistry and refined sophistication.

> With each thoughtful *renovation*, La Mamounia beautifully *preserves* its allure, showcasing the exquisite Arabo-Andalusian heritage

The restaurant Le Marocain offers a serene ambiance where cuisine artfully bridges tradition and innovation.

Oriental Living

Oriental Living

La Mamounia's interiors showcase Moroccan *artistry*, with intricate *sculpting, molding,* and *painting* by skilled local artisans

Through the ornately decorated doors, a luxurious bedroom unfolds, exuding refined elegance. The intricate patterns frame a serene space where a lavish bed with an exquisitely carved headboard takes center stage. Rich textures and plush furnishings blend harmoniously, creating a sanctuary of comfort and style for an unparalleled retreat.

Its renovations have continuously celebrated and rejuvenated the Arabo-Andalusian architectural heritage and the Moroccan way of life, crafted to perfection by local artisans. For generations, these skilled "Maalems" have dedicated themselves to the traditional crafts of sculpting, molding, shaping, chiseling, and painting, weaving together intricate lines and patterns that showcase the exquisite Moroccan art that La Mamounia displays in its full glory.

Materials such as wood, tadelakt, zellige, plaster, nickel silver, copper and leather are exalted here, captivating visitors with the stunningly adorned lounges and bedrooms. The latest transformation, spanning three years under the guidance of Jacques Garcia, was a labor of love that refreshed the Grande Dame's elegance while preserving its essence. A dedicated team of one hundred artisans was engaged, utilizing 73,000 meters of taffeta, velvet and silk brocade, meticulously adorned its spaces.

The exclusive Mamounia fragrance, crafted by Olivia Giacobetti, adds another layer of allure, enhancing the ambience for romantic evenings. With 135 rooms, 71 suites, and 3 riads, La Mamounia stands ready to embrace those enchanted by Marrakech's charm.

Gebs, zellige and wood: each door at La Mamounia, numbering 2,264, serves as a portal to wonder, toggling between openness and mystery.

As the sun sets, La Mamounia transforms into a captivating spectacle of light and shadow, its architecture and gardens taking on an ethereal glow. This enchanting setting becomes the backdrop for unforgettable moments, whether it's a tranquil evening stroll through the aromatic gardens, a sumptuous dinner under the stars, or simply reveling in its tranquil beauty. Each corner tells a story, each space extends an invitation to experience the magic of Marrakech in unparalleled luxury. La Mamounia not only stands as a testament to Moroccan elegance and craftsmanship but also serves as a sanctuary where the spirit of Marrakech thrives, beckoning guests to immerse themselves in its timeless beauty and serene luxury. —

Churchill Suite: Churchill's name above the bed in Arabic script creates a decor that blends English style with Moroccan art.

The Gem of Marrakech

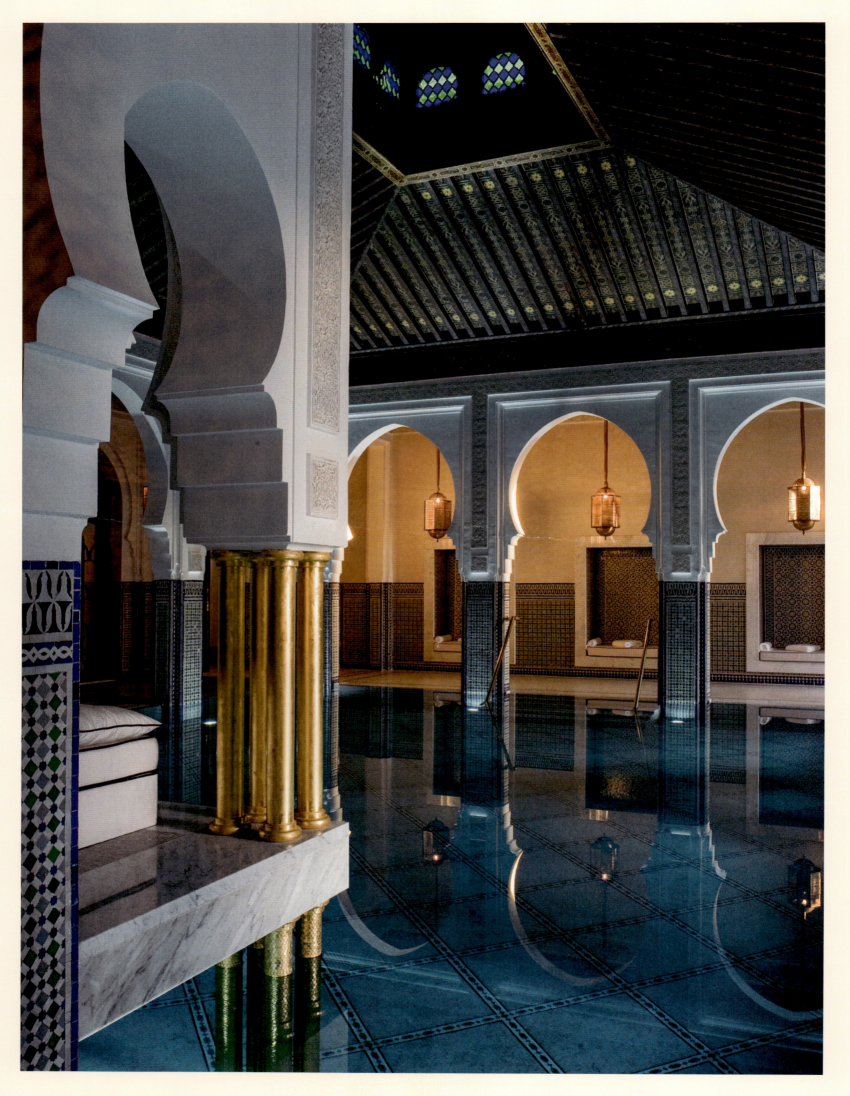

Arches mirrored in the pool pay homage to the grand Ménara basin, with 750 square meters of Italian marble and 1,200 cubic meters of water setting the stage for indulgent spa experiences.

(next page) In the past, La Mamounia was a place where savoir faire was more than art, it was a philosophy.

Spirit of the Past

—·⟫⟪·—

Collector, self-taught painter and designer Henry Loussian is so passionate about Beirut's historic houses that he has spent over a decade constructing his very own heritage home, known as Musée Henry.

In the Batroun heights, amidst mountains and orchards, Henry Loussian has built the house of his dreams: a traditional Beirut home, meticulously crafted from elements salvaged from 45 demolished buildings in Beirut. Our dedicated collector acquired arches, cornices, marble pillars, and cement tiles, piece by piece. Despite facing financial constraints, his determination paved the way for the miraculous materialisation of financial resources, allowing the past to weave into the future.

Henry honed a myriad of skills—masonry, painting, ironworking, cabinet-making, architecture—day by day. Living by the adage "practice makes perfect," he embodies this principle. Undeterred and with relentless energy, he meticulously assembled the pieces of his grand vision, positioning stones, beams, windows and floors as if solving a huge puzzle. Gradually, his project rose from its foundations, evolving into a magnificent palace mirroring those he had diligently captured in photographs over the years,

Nestled amidst lush greenery, this house turned museum exudes Lebanese charm with its pastel façade and terracotta roofs. The vibrant shutters and elegant balconies add a touch of whimsy, inviting one to explore the beauty hidden within its walls and the tranquil nature that surrounds it. Perfectly blending with its environment, it stands as a serene retreat from the bustling world.

(left) This grand hall dazzles with ornate ceilings and intricate stained glass, centered by a majestic chandelier that casts soft light over polished marble floors, reflecting opulent design and architectural finesse.

(below) An inviting nook with detailed ceiling artwork and a colorful stained-glass partition provides a cozy spot for relaxation overlooking lush greenery outside.

Oriental Living

Every element is perfectly positioned. The chandeliers from Basta harmonise beautifully with the ceiling paintings, adding a touch of elegance. The linen-draped sofa, adorned with embroidered fabric, is complemented by a charming fish cushion.

Henry Loussian meticulously *assembled* his dream place atop the Batroun heights, using salvaged elements from 45 *demolished buildings* in Beirut, crafting a traditional home from the past

incorporating all the materials he had lovingly restored. The final touches adorned the ceilings with hand-painted frescoes in the traditional manner. Transitioning from a jewelry designer to a master of illumination, Loussian crafted idyllic scenes and intricate floral designs, drawing inspiration from historic ceilings and their depictions in *Byzance* magazine. Despite the challenging nature of the task and the occasional deviations from his vision by craftsmen, his determination never wavered. His commitment to authenticity ensured that every element, including the œil-de-bœuf windows, served not merely for decoration but retained their historical function of lighting and ventilation. The design of the ceilings, the layout of the rooms, and the architectural details all adhered to this meticulous approach, ensuring that every aspect remained true to its historical inspiration.

The outcome is breathtaking. Loussian's endeavor has surpassed his wildest dreams, with the allure of bygone days bestowing upon him a gift so royal, he made his creation his home. The space eschews excess furnishings or glittering adornments; instead, a selection of chairs, an armchair, cabinets, tables and strategically placed cushions narrate tales of antiquity. The living room emerges as a sanctuary bathed in light, where each object, reimagined by our artist, finds new purpose. The handcrafted screen of colored glass, an armchair swathed in linen, cushions embroidered with care,

Oriental Living

The trio of doors, crowned with arches, have been expertly resized to enhance the beauty of the surroundings. The addition of plants, lanterns and ceiling frescoes brings the finishing touches to the space.

Spirit of the Past

Braided straw trays, carafes, and a soft blue cupboard, all discovered in Basta, come together to evoke a nostalgia-filled kitchen.

and an arrangement of low tables beside lanterns, basins and verdant plants—all elements coalesce in a symphony of simplicity and precision placement.

The bathroom now boasts a fully restored glass mosaic window, enhancing its charm. Throughout the residence, once uninspired doors and windows have been transformed with the introduction of skylights, archways and marble pillars, infusing each space with character and vitality. A striking display of Vuitton suitcases at the foot of the bed is a testament to Loussian's unwavering dedication to his artistic journey. His storerooms are brimming with materials, poised for the revival of numerous other dwellings. Similarly, his Ashrafieh apartment is evolving, embodying his steadfast belief in the power of dreams. —

Spirit of the Past

This bathroom features a classic clawfoot tub set against a backdrop of vibrant stained-glass windows. The intricate lanterns add a touch of old-world charm, while the surrounding tiles and greenery enhance the space's tranquil ambiance.

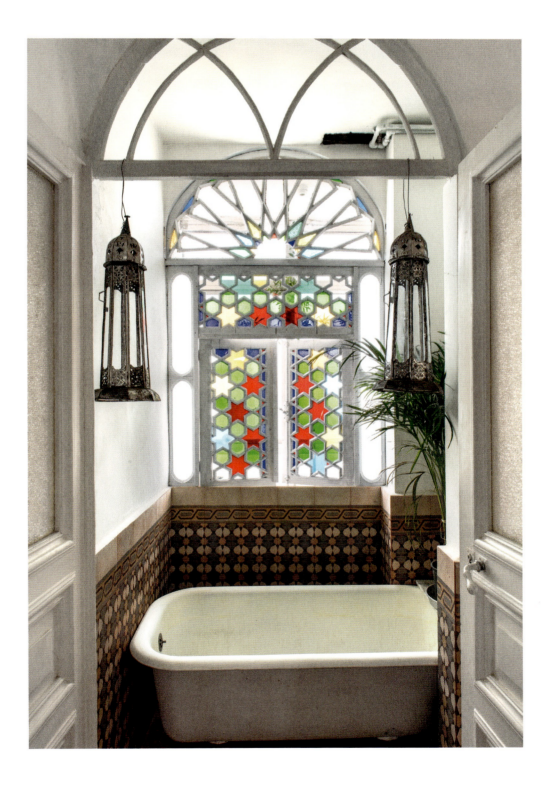

Oriental Living

Throughout the residence, once uninspired doors and windows have been transformed with the introduction of *skylights*, *archways* and *marble pillars*, infusing each space with *character* and *vitality*

A cozy corner, complete with a classic cabinet and eclectic décor, a plush armchair, and a vibrant rug, creating a perfect spot for quiet reflection or leisurely afternoons.

Spirit of the Past

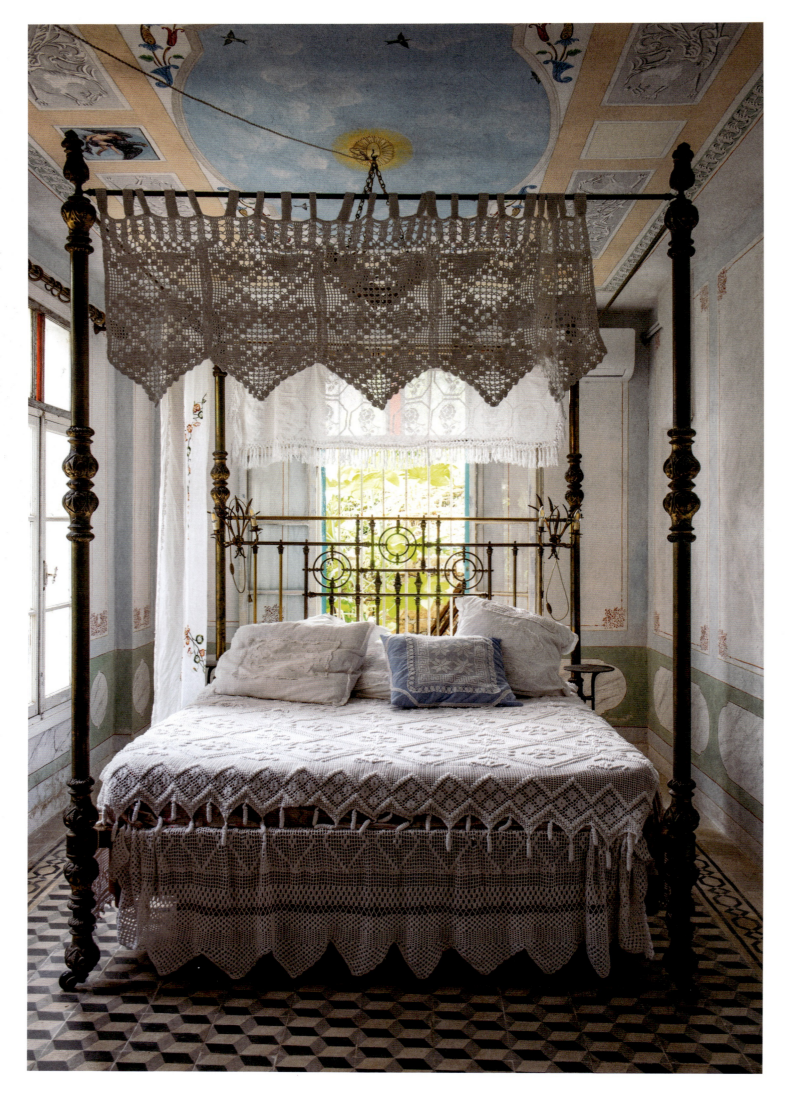

(left) This enchanting bedroom showcases a regal four-poster bed draped with lace under a sky-painted ceiling, surrounded by floral wall designs and ornate window ironwork, creating a vintage romantic retreat.

(above) Stone walls and arched doorways contrast with sleek white chairs and a contemporary table, offering a unique, well-lit space for gatherings, enhanced by a classic chandelier.

Henry's determination and creativity allowed him to transform *financial constraints* into a *magnificent palace* that blends historical authenticity with modern *functionality*

(above) Through an ornate marble archway adorned with a classic chandelier and intricate iron transom, this corridor opens into a sunlit nook framed by stained glass and architectural details. Richly colored rugs lead to comfortable seating, vibrant cushions, and lush greenery, creating a tranquil space.

(right) The exterior door retains its nostalgic allure, beckoning us on a journey through time. Cement tiles and sequences of corridors set the stage for the exploration ahead.

Every room in Henry's creation features elements that blend *historical inspiration* with modern *functionality*, creating a breathtaking and *harmonious* living space

Oriental Living

Urban Loft

Choosing to orient oneself away from the sea to embrace the urban landscape was, undoubtedly, a daring move. The renowned architect, Bernard Khoury, has outdone himself in this endeavor: a ninth-floor penthouse in the NBK Residence, and his home since 2012. Adhering to precise lines and ratios, he meticulously crafted each aspect to custom specifications, akin to the precision found in haute couture fashion.

Mastering the art of concealment: Bernard Khoury opts for matte black over traditional white, transforming plaster into a modern marvel. A swing, a hanging bridge—it's almost poetic. Unlocking these double-level doors, you're greeted with an unparalleled sense of liberation.

(next page) In the living room, the 6m-tall bookshelves and French oak wood paneling were handmade by local artisans., Furnishings include a 'Fifty' armchair from Ligne Roset and a 'Lui 5/A' armchair by Philippe Bestenheider for Fratelli Boffi.

"Upon being presented with this location, I seized the opportunity immediately! We're situated at a pivotal point in Beirut, a city lacking a unified urban plan. Our surroundings are akin to isolated islands, each a standalone institution: the Faculty of Medicine, the French Embassy, the Pine Forest, the Maronite Cemetery... This unique positioning offers unparalleled urban views, a vantage point I preferred over the sea. I desired a home that directly engages with the city's chaotic expansion, offering a sanctuary amidst its tumult, a home that is neither overly romantic nor overly sweet, but fully integrated with the urban landscape," Bernard Khoury said, gesturing towards the haphazard mix of buildings below. From this perspective, the complex urban fabric of Beirut's past and present somehow becomes appealing.

Precision in every detail: from floor to ceiling, including the ventilation and heating systems, every aspect harmonises with its environment.

Oriental Living

Urban Loft

The precision and *craftsmanship* in Bernard Khoury's urban loft, from detailed *woodwork* to *metalwork*, celebrate exceptional local artisanship, blending materials seamlessly for optimal air circulation and *energy efficiency*

When entering Khoury's "perched house," as he fondly refers to his loft towering above Beirut, one is immediately struck by the precision of the design. Every element, from the architecture to the minutiae of the door handles, adheres to a meticulously planned design ethos. It's the hallmark of an architectural maestro. The space, enveloped in wood, offers the serene isolation of a bird in a baobab tree, indifferent to the chaos below. It serves as a powerful lesson in contrasts, a testament to a uniquely Lebanese duality.

The residence spans three levels. The first floor houses the living room, dining area, kitchen, and master bedroom. The second level is dedicated to the children's suites, while the third accommodates a guest bedroom and staff quarters. The rooftop swimming pool, offering a 360-degree view of Beirut, is a luxurious oasis framed by olive trees, epitomizing ultimate relaxation.

"The main living space is defined by a large, south-facing opening, twelve meters wide and seven meters deep, carefully designed to maintain privacy," the homeowner explains. He adds, "My grandfather's craftsmanship as a carpenter inspired me to take on the challenge of the detailed woodwork in this house. The artisan responsible for it has been with our family since I was born, spanning three generations. He's the one who crafted the dining room table." The wooden slats cleverly conceal heating units and storage, blending seamlessly with the surrounding steelwork, allowing for optimal air circulation and energy efficiency. —

This stunning spiral staircase is a testament to the home's meticulous craftsmanship and design. With its seamless blend of wood and steel, it elegantly winds upward, creating a visually captivating centerpiece that connects the various levels of the house. Each step is a harmonious fusion of form and function, reflecting Bernard Khoury's dedication to precision and beauty.

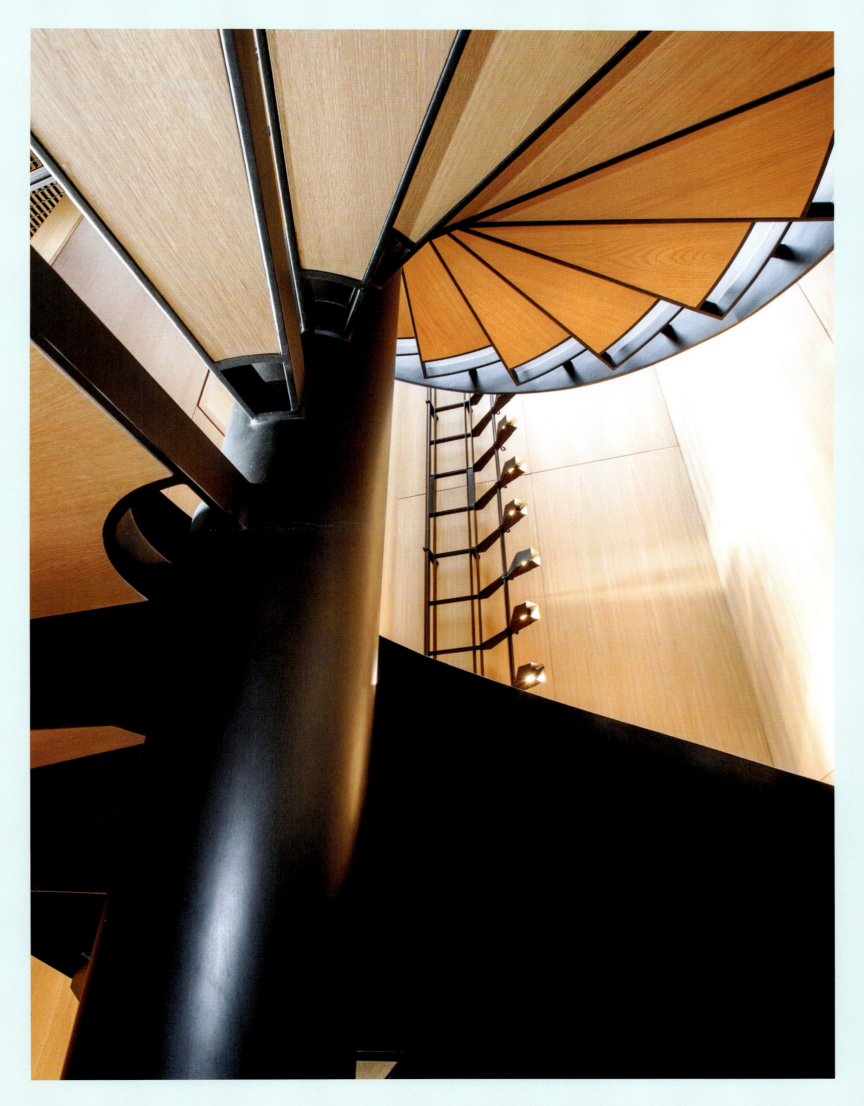

Urban Loft

Oriental Living

(above) An artistic touch elevates this modern living space, where a sleek, geometric side table supports a sculptural hand, adding intrigue and personality.

(left) A tranquil retreat within the home, this bathroom exudes serenity and elegance. The freestanding bathtub, framed by soft, flowing curtains, invites relaxation.

The precision and craftsmanship in the metalwork mirror the quality found in the woodwork, showcasing a perfect blend of materials and craftsmanship, courtesy of the company Acid. "In each of my projects, I strive to celebrate the exceptional local craftsmanship that is increasingly overlooked in favor of cheaper, imported alternatives, which undermines the value of handcrafted, quality work."

The ceiling stands as another homage to Lebanese craftsmanship. Eschewing a conventional false ceiling, Khoury collaborated with a seasoned 75-year-old artisan to create a plaster masterpiece in matte black, innovatively designed for optimal air distribution and a stark departure from traditional white ceilings. A noteworthy feature is the bridge encircling the library, ingeniously concealing the structural elements between two glass bays. Opening these sides offers an illusion of floating above the cityscape, merging structural ingenuity with the essence of urban living. —

Oriental Living

The Art and the Way

—⋅≫ ≪⋅—

In Beirut's pulsing heart, interior designer Ramy Boutros masterfully reimagined an apartment, striking a perfect architectural harmony that enhances room proportions, facilitates seamless flow among spaces, and introduces elements of surprise in every corner through unique shapes and materials.

From the main entrance to this apartment which is located in a contemporary tower, instead of hitting a straight wall, Ramy Boutros designed an organic oval shape which leads both to the bedrooms or to the reception room which has a view on the sea.

The journey to the bedrooms is marked by an enchanting corridor adorned with a sequence of French oak doors. These doors, enhanced with modern Chinese lacquer, frame the central attraction: an Édouard Lièvre-designed piece adorned with a Japanese clock.

In the dining-room, a striking five-meter-long black lacquered dining table designed by Ramy Boutros captivates with its seemingly levitating top supported by sculptural legs, infusing a classic setting with modern flair.

From the vivid strokes of Nabil Nahas's 'Untitled' (2022) in acrylic on wood, to the evocative 'Dream 115' (2015) by Safwan Dahoul at Ayyam Gallery, Lebanon. Delving into craftsmanship with a pair of circa 1900 English-French mahogany open armchairs adorned with embossed leather top rails, alongside an elegant guéridon featuring a golden and patinated bronze monogram, its base graced by three seated pharaohs.

(previous page) Early 19th-century neoclassical vases meet Nabil Nahas's vibrant 'Vesuvius II' (2023). The ensemble is crowned by a majestic neo-Egyptian chair, intricately inlaid with wood and ivory, alongside the sleek elegance of Macassar wood Mallet chairs—a fusion of history, art and design.

(right) Dive into the abstract depths with two untitled acrylic masterpieces on wood by Nabil Nahas (2022), and Samia Halaby's serene 'Morning Light in the Desert' (2013) from Ayyam Gallery, Lebanon. Explore functional art with Mattia Bonetti's candlesticks from David Gill Gallery, London, and the limited-edition 'Shanghai Chaise Num.388' (2012) by Hervé Van der Straeten, alongside Safwan Dahoul's contemplative 'Dream 56' (2012). Completing the collection, Mark Brazier-Jones's amethyst tables from Michèle Hayem Gallery, France, merge natural beauty with artistic craftsmanship.

Oriental Living

This scene is complemented by Christian Liaigre's wooden and black leather chairs, while chinoiserie-themed screens and sleek lacquered panels set against 19th-century furnishings amplify the decor's elegance. Contrasting black-and-white artwork injects a contemporary vibe, further enriched by architecture that beautifully ties the room together.

It must be admitted that Ramy Boutros transforms everything he touches into a magical universe. He dares and creates unexpected combinations. His great passion, the exoticism dreamed of by Europeans: Egyptomania, Japonism and French Chinoiserie... As a perfect conjurer, he wallpapers the walls with all these dreams of the Orient, adding contemporary paintings. This is absolutely the case in this apartment where all objects converse without a false note. And we see Austrian chairs from the 1920s which discuss in complete harmony with a table which tells of the craze for Egyptomania, following Bonaparte's campaign in 1799. The same language brought by the portrait of Safwan Dahoul made in a contemporary pharaonic spirit. The modern paintings by Nabil Nahas complete the whole by adding the essential touch of color. All in a setting made of moldings and woodwork that you absolutely wouldn't expect. Finally, on the floor, a checkerboard tile which uses old pink, yellow and white to match the tones of the apartment rather than the classic black and white.

André Dubreuil's unique console (2014), a striking blend of bronze, stainless steel and copper with green lacquer, showcased at David Gill Gallery, London. Complementing this masterpiece, the 'Bougeoir Flamme No.325' (2006) by Hervé Van der Straeten, a testament to French elegance and innovative design, presented by Gallery France.

Instead of hitting a straight wall, Ramy Boutros designed an *organic oval* shape which leads both to the *bedrooms*

(below) The bespoke 'Pebble' dining table by Ramy Boutros, a fusion of contemporary design with natural inspiration. Seats by Christian Liaigre. Paired with the exquisite craftsmanship of a Japonism-style clock by L'Escalier de Cristal, and the intricate beauty of an 1881-1886 Armoire Japonisante by Edouard Lièvre, a masterpiece in rosewood with golden bronze decor and a red griotte marble top from Steinitz Gallery, France. A celebration of cultural artistry and timeless design.

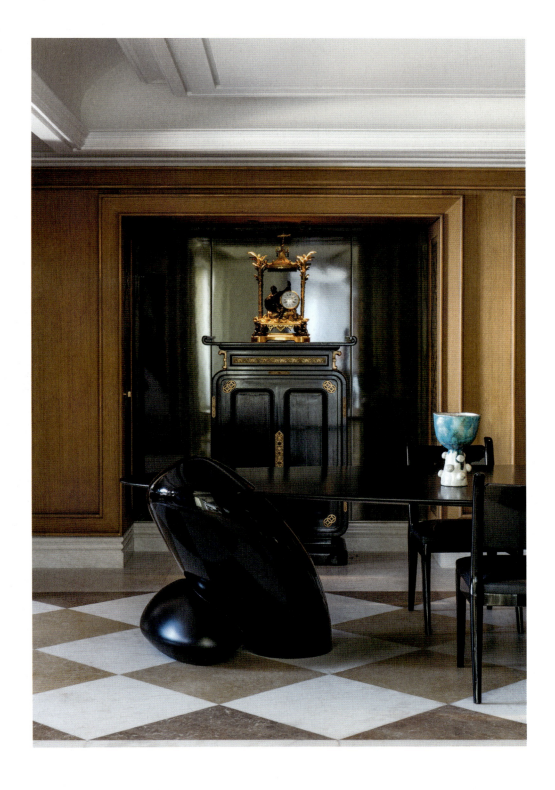

Oriental Living

'Marilyn VS Brigitte' by Alex Guofeng CAO, a captivating chromogenic print encased in Dibond Plexiglass from Villa del Arte Gallery, Barcelona, juxtaposes iconic beauty through intricate imagery. Complementing this visual dialogue, customized bars by Ramy Boutros, with their sleek lacquered metal and marble tops, blend functionality with elegance, creating spaces that are as stylish as they are inviting.

The Art and the Way

Oriental Living

It must be admitted that Ramy Boutros *transforms* everything he touches into a *magical universe.* He dares and creates *unexpected* combinations

(left) Edouard Agneesens's 'Geisha with a Fan and Butterflies' brings 19th-century charm, paired with Ferdinand Barbedienne's exquisite Champlevé enamel cache pot on an onyx base. The ensemble is beautifully completed by a Japonisante table, inspired by Edouard Lièvre's designs, blending Eastern motifs with European craftsmanship for a timeless cultural fusion.

(right) Montse Valdés's '27-3-2012', an oil on canvas that captures the essence of contemporary emotion and color at Villa del Arte Gallery, Barcelona. Complementing this piece, a customized Art Déco bar by Ramy Boutros, where sleek design meets functional sophistication, creating a space of unparalleled style and allure.

Ghassan Zard Abou Jaoudé's mixed media on canvas (2012) presents a vibrant exploration of texture and form. This dynamic expression is complemented by the sleek sophistication of a Minotti bed, offering a refined aesthetic. The ensemble is illuminated by the whimsical elegance of Hubert Le Gall's creations: the 'Marguerite' tables and 'Odilon' chandelier from Gallery France, each piece a testament to innovative design and artistic craftsmanship.

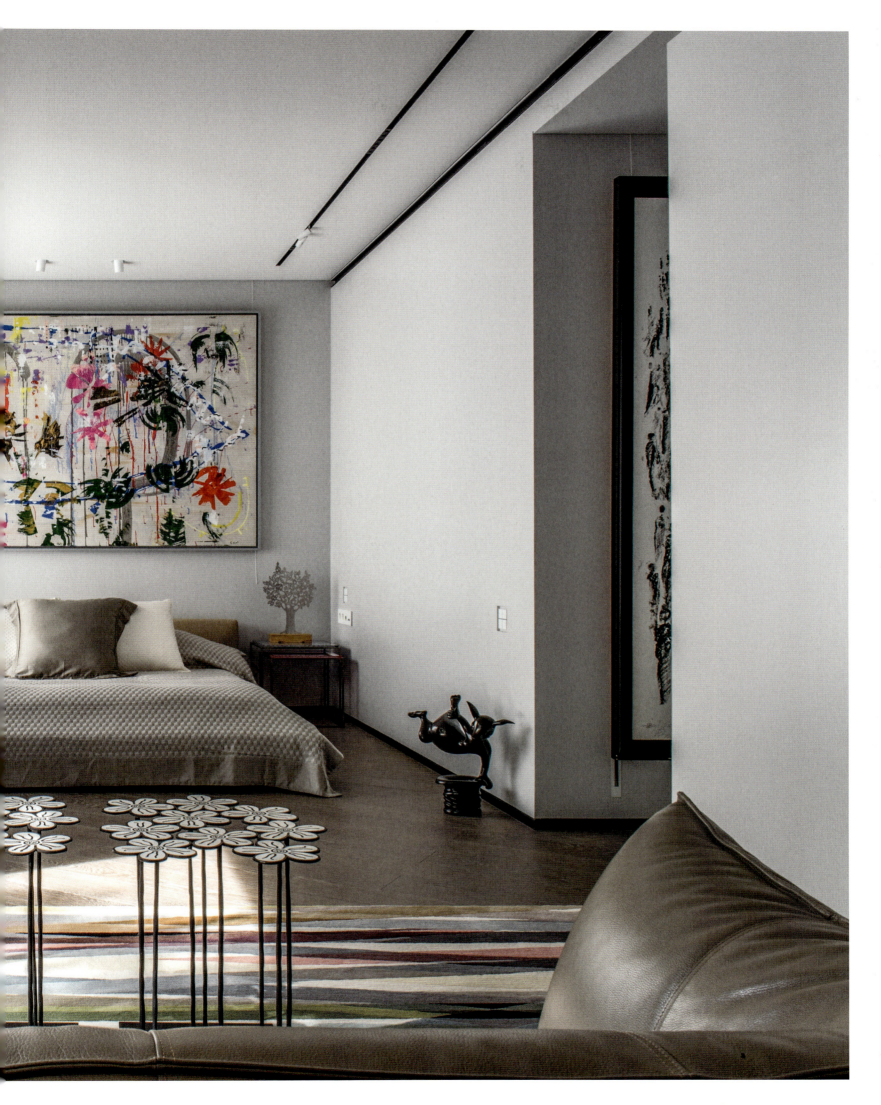

Ramy's goal, above all, is to offer a *setting* where any object can be *placed with beauty*

It is clear that the mix and match practiced in this place is great art. You have to dare to mix such objects! However, isn't that the best way to tell the story of the inhabitants of a place, especially when they are inveterate collectors? And to think that Ramy Boutros denies being a decorator. For him, the important thing is first and foremost that the house looks beautiful empty and that the materials used can age gracefully. In his architecture, he does not rely at all on the choice of furniture. Its goal, above all, is to offer a setting where any object can be placed with beauty. Indeed, experience has proven to him more than once that tastes and desires evolve over time. His designs cater to clients' dreams and expectations on every level—from architecture and object placement to material selection and spatial quality, aiming to craft lifestyles rather than just spaces. His expertise lies in tailoring the client's lifestyle, starting with crafting an architecture that is harmonious and well-proportioned, complemented by strategic lighting. He selects materials that gracefully mature alongside the occupants, ensuring the space is captivating, whether furnished or not. For him, the essence of design transcends just furniture; it's about creating an environment where each piece feels at home within a beautifully illuminated and proportioned space. —

This sleek and minimalist workspace is designed to inspire creativity and focus. The striking blue geometric rug anchors the room, providing a bold contrast to the clean white walls and cabinets. A modern wooden desk serves as the centerpiece, adorned with eclectic decor, including a classical bust and sculptural element.

(above) A striking red console table with a reflective circular base, creating a stunning focal point. The dynamic design is complemented by a unique patterned rug that adds texture and movement to the space.

(right) This luxurious hallway showcases intricate wooden paneling and ornate doors, each adorned with elaborate detailing. The checkered floor pattern adds a touch of classic elegance, guiding visitors towards a beautifully crafted focal point at the end of the corridor.

The journey to the bedrooms is marked by an *enchanting corridor* adorned with a sequence of French *oak doors*

Oriental Living

TEXT
Désirée Sadek

PHOTOGRAPHY
Guillaume de Laubier

BOOK DESIGN
Han van de Ven

Sign up for our newsletter with news about new and forthcoming publications on art, interior design, food & travel, photography and fashion as well as exclusive offers and events. If you have any questions or comments about the material in this book, please do not hesitate to contact our editorial team: art@lannoo.com

©Lannoo Publishers, Belgium, 2024
ISBN: 978-94-014-2244-4
NUR 454/450 D/2024/45/406
www.lannoo.com

All rights reserved. No part of this publication may be reproduced or transmitted in any form or by any means, electronic or mechanical, including photography, recording or any other information storage and retrieval system, without prior permission in writing from the publisher. Every effort has been made to trace copyright holders. If, however, you feel that you have inadvertently been overlooked, please contact the publishers.

Oriental Living

— ❯❯❮❮ —

Step into a world where history and modernity dance in perfect harmony. *Oriental Living* is a captivating exploration of the exquisite beauty and rich cultural heritage of the Middle East, masterfully interwoven with contemporary design.

Marvel at the intricate craftsmanship and artistic traditions that have defined Oriental design for centuries. Explore how antique treasures and modern elements blend to create spaces that are both nostalgic and forward-thinking. Delve into a realm, where ancient history and contemporary creativity coexist in stunning harmony. From tranquil retreats to bustling urban sanctuaries, each featured home offers a unique story of cultural fusion and personal expression.

With breathtaking photography by Guillaume de Laubier and insightful texts by Désirée Sadek, *Oriental Living* invites you on a journey through spaces where every room tells a story, and every story enriches the tapestry of Oriental art and design.

Whether you are a lover of interior design, a history enthusiast, or simply someone who appreciates the beauty of cultural heritage, this book will inspire and captivate, offering a deeper connection to the timeless elegance and modern allure of Oriental living.

www.lannoo.com